Jane Bowen

From Triumph to Tragedy

The Story of the Paddle Steamer *Pegasus* and her people 1835–1843

novum ◢ pro

This book is also
available as
e-book.

www.novum-publishing.co.uk

© 2021 novum publishing

ISBN 978-3-99107-708-4
Editing: Hugo Chandler, BA
Cover photos: Ekaterina Gerasimova,
Grian12, Rodjulian | Dreamstime.com
Cover design, layout & typesetting:
novum publishing
Internal illustrations: See list of illustrations and maps on page 16–18

The author's moral rights have been
asserted.

The images provided by the author
have been printed in the highest
possible quality.

www.novum-publishing.co.uk

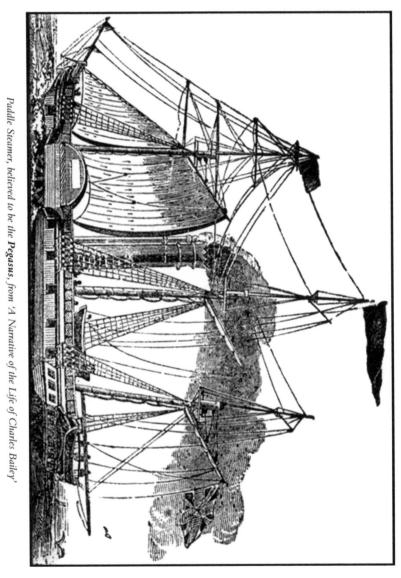

*Paddle Steamer, believed to be the **Pegasus**, from 'A Narrative of the Life of Charles Bailey'*

For Janet, who has shared
the search for the *Pegasus*,
and without whose encouragement,
and research and photographic skills,
this book would never have
been completed.

CONTENTS

FOREWORD

The story of the steam ship *Pegasus* is probably not one well known to many people. It was built in the 1830s for the coastal sea route from Leith to Hull, at a time when steamships were seen as an improvement on the speed and reliability of sailing ships. For many it was preferable to a long uncomfortable journey by coach, assuming it wasn't a stormy sea!

I first became aware of the ship and its sinking off Holy Island in the 1990s, when a couple of people visited the Berwick Record Office looking for information. I knew the name of the ship but not the story behind it and could only provide access to the local newspaper, *Berwick Advertiser*. Over the years, I have picked up more bits of information-entries in the Bamburgh and Holy Island burial registers; the badly worn gravestone dedicated to Field Flowers in Holy Island Churchyard and the programme on comedian, Sarah Millican in 'Who Do You Think You Are', where it was revealed that one of her ancestors had worked on the wreck as a diver. However, these were only bits and pieces, only part of the story.

When Jane asked me to read her book, I was very keen to do this as I wanted to know what she had found out. As Jane is an avid and meticulous researcher, I knew she would leave no nook or cranny unturned in her quest for information. The book hasn't disappointed and I have been amazed about what is revealed not only about the boat, the company who ran it and its sad fate on what was really a clear night but in very dangerous waters. However, this is only half the picture, as what really brings this book to life is the previously untold stories of those on board, most of whom were lost and many whose bodies were never recovered. I was fascinated to read about their diverse backgrounds and this book is really a testament and legacy for them and what local and family history is all about – ordinary people and places and how their lives become intertwined with events which shaped the future of shipping.

Who would have thought that a chance discovery of some information in an archive would lead to such detailed and varied research on a little-known disaster off the Northumberland coast, which deserves to be properly recorded and remembered, a fitting memorial to those involved with it.

Linda Bankier, Berwick Archivist

PREFACE

My interest in the *Pegasus* began when I found, in the Northumberland Archives, a collection of proofs of 'Reward' notices, looking for information about passengers lost following the sinking of the *Pegasus* in July 1843. The number of different notices suggested a serious disaster, but I had never heard of it. I was curious.

A Google search produced accounts of the disaster, in its day the worst merchant marine disaster in British waters. In the search, I also found that the company records were held in the Glasgow University Archives. From the information there, and in the British Newspaper Archives, a much fuller picture of the ship and its activities began to emerge.

Built in 1835, specifically for the Leith/Hull route, at the time the *Pegasus* was at the cutting edge of ship design – and a forerunner of John Masefield's 'Dirty British coaster'. In the years that followed, the weekly passenger and goods service she provided was a key link in the industrialisation of Scotland before railway communication was fully established. In each country, she created markets for goods produced by other countries. At a time when political revolutions were still current in Europe, the service contributed to the security of the United Kingdom as a whole, allowing troops to be moved efficiently to garrisons across the country. The *Pegasus* also had a hand in the entertainments industry of the day. Racehorses, theatre companies and menageries all sailed on her, making travelling shows accessible to a much wider audience.

Her unexpected wreck, on a clear summer's night in 1843, shocked the nation, and left grieving families across Britain, from Inverness to London, and Wales to Lincolnshire. Even then, she was at the forefront of salvage activity, with some of the first deep sea helmeted divers working on her to retrieve bodies and goods. From the disaster, and the enquiries which followed, came the beginnings of better shipping regulation.

This is the story I have tried to tell – I hope you will find it as fascinating as I have.

ACKNOWLEDGEMENTS

This book would not have been possible without the help, encouragement and advice of those who generously shared their own work and research with me. Particular thanks are due to:

Judith Fawcett Armstrong; Linda Bankier (Berwick-upon-Tweed Record Office), Ann Bevan (The Historical Diving Society), John Bevan (Holy Island), Michael Finchen (The Quartermaster's Store), Alexander Findlater, the late Ron French, Norman Frisby and Graham Knox (St. Chad's Church, Rochdale), Jill Groves, Louise Harrison (London Metropolitan Archives), Kathryn Jones (Lincolnshire Archives), Eva La Pensée, Ervine Long, Bill Longbone, June Slee, Philip Somervail, Wendy and Alan Urwin, and Lisa Waters (Bamburgh Castle Archives).

LIST OF ILLUSTRATIONS AND MAPS

ILLUSTRATIONS

MAPS

Part 1

SAILING THE LEITH/HULL ROUTE

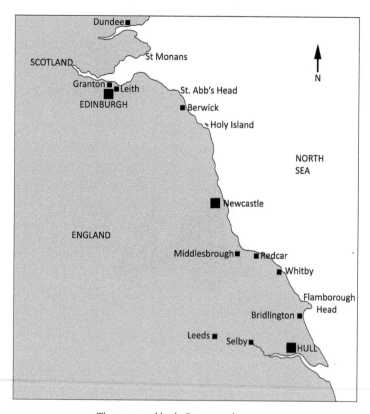

*The area covered by the **Pegasus** on her voyages*

CHAPTER 1

THE BARCLAY FAMILY SHIPWRIGHTS

Glasgow 1818; Britain's twenty-year war with France was over. With peace had come new developments. In Glasgow, a key feature of this was the growth in shipping. Apart from the revival of industry, several other things contributed also. At a time when water rather than road was the most efficient form of transport, good access was critical.

Until the end of the 18th century, most Glasgow bound ships had docked at the appropriately named Port Glasgow, or Greenock; both over twenty miles away, because the Clyde was too shallow and twisting to let them sail up to Glasgow. During the war years, however, the establishment of jetties along the banks of the Clyde had narrowed and deepened the channel, and a dredging machine worked by seven men helped make the river navigable for larger ships up to the city harbour at the Broomielaw. Before the war, only 40-ton ships could dock at the city, but now 100-ton vessels could make the journey, and trade had risen from some 56,000 tons per annum to 141,000 tons. The ability to sail between Glasgow and Edinburgh on the Forth and Clyde Canal attracted even more shipping into Glasgow. Further encouragement was given when, in 1817 and 1818, the Government allowed the establishment of bonded warehouses in the city. This did away with the need to pay duty immediately to both Customs and Excise Officers before goods could be unloaded. The delays which this caused, had been a considerable deterrent to both merchants and shippers. The difference it made can be judged from the duty collected. Whereas in 1800, only £460 had been collected in duty, by 1820 the figure was £11,428.

Overall, it was a time of opportunity, and among those ready to seize the chance was John Barclay and his sons, Thomas and Robert. John Barclay seems to have been born around 1775, possibly in Port Glasgow. He is thought to have trained as a carpenter, and certainly his son, Robert was apprenticed to him as a carpenter; possibly also his elder brother Thomas, although Thomas went on to be an auctioneer. The first records of John, in Glasgow, describe him as a manufacturer, and then as a merchant, dealing apparently in tobacco and clay pipes. In 1818, however, he began boatbuilding on the north side of the Clyde at the Broomielaw, running his business from his house in York Street. Five years later, he leased two and a quarter acres of land at Stobcross to create a shipbuilding and repair yard. The chosen site, sloping gradually towards the river, was at a point where the water was deep and wide enough for large ships to be launched. In many ways, however, the repair element of the business was the more important. John built a slip or means of drawing ships out of the water for repair, at the time there were no dry docks, and this was the only such facility on the upper Clyde, well positioned to meet the needs of the growing numbers of vessels coming to the city.

A slip dock on the River Clyde 1827, possibly Barclays' at Stobcross by permission of University of Glasgow Library, Archives & Special Collections, James Hopkirk

This picture, drawn on or before 1827, shows the slip in use for repairing a wooden sailing smack. Ships were pulled out of the water with the aid of a windlass. This enabled damaged hulls to be repaired and re-tarred to make them watertight, the process which seems to be going on in the picture – note the two men heating the tar over a fire on the riverbank. The slip was also used to clean the hulls. Just as cars today need to be serviced to run efficiently, so at this time, ships needed their hulls cleaned of growths which would accumulate on voyages, most commonly seaweeds and barnacles, and which if not removed would slow the ship in the water. Wooden ships sailing in warmer waters were also liable to be attacked by ships' worms. Before the French wars, the Navy had pioneered the use of copper plating on ships' hulls to protect the wood from attack. Although the process was costly, by the end of the war this process was increasingly being adopted by merchant shipping. John's slip could be used for this work. The development of the slip is a good indication of John's opportunism. He recognised a gap in the market and took steps to fill it. It also demonstrates another aspect of his opportunism. In March 1824, Thomas Morton, a Leith shipbuilder, took John Barclay's Stobcross Shipwright Company to court for infringing his 1818 patent (valid for fourteen years) on machinery, for use when pulling ships out of water on a slip, and claimed £500 damages. The Barclays did not contest the action. They were fortunate that the Lord Chief Commissioner, who heard the action, decided that the complainant had not shown he had suffered damage as a result of the infringement. The jury were directed to find in Morton's favour, but to award only token damages. As a result, the Barclays had to pay damages of one shilling, but also the costs of the action.

At this time, the *Glasgow Post Office Directory* shows John's business interests thus:

- » Barclay, John, & Co. boat builders, 29, Broomielaw; slip for repairs, Finnieston; office, 15, York street
- » Barclay, John, ship carpenter, house, 15, York street

Other records show that John was also a Burgess and Guild Brother of Glasgow, a respected member of the City community.

John may have seen a great opportunity, but sadly his timing was not quite right. By the end of 1825, the Stobcross Shipwright Company was in financial difficulties, probably due to too few ships using the repair facilities. Even if experiencing problems, most ships' masters would prefer to get their vessels, themselves and their crews back to their home port if possible. In April 1826, the Stobcross Yard was advertised for sale in the *Glasgow Herald*:

SHIP-BUILDING CONCERN.
FOR SALE, BY PRIVATE BARGAIN,

THE YARD at STOBCROSS, a little West of the Broomielaw, with the Slip, Erections, &c. thereon. The Slip affords room for three vessels to repair; there is room and trade for another, which may hold more and of larger tonnage, besides ample accommodation for every branch connected with Ship-building. The trade of Glasgow has been progressively increasing, and the improvements on the River hold out a certain prospect of its accelerated continuance.

Such a property is rarely to be met with, having peculiar privileges and advantages, besides offering a most favourable opportunity for carrying on an extended business. The Premises are most excellently calculated for building and repairing vessels, or for connecting the Engineer business with Ship and Steam-boat Building, as there is room for constructing a Dock for putting in Machinery without interfering with the Carpenter's Slips. Such a business, from its connection with the Harbour, would command a preference from the great saving of time to Steam Vessels requiring repairs of both Boat and Engine.

For further particulars, apply to John Barclay, No. 15, York Street, or at the Works.

Glasgow, 6th April, 1826

In June and August 1826, there were unsuccessful attempts to sell the property by public auction. Then on 11 November 1826, John Barclay 'merchant and tobacco-pipe maker in Glasgow, and also carrying on business as a carpenter at Stobcross, near Glasgow, under the firm of THE STOBCROSS SHIP-WRIGHT COMPANY' applied to be made bankrupt. All the estates of both John himself and of the Stobcross Shipwright Company were sequestered, but when the notice to appoint commissioners for his bankruptcy was drawn up on 20 December 1826, John was recorded as dead.

What happened to John is a mystery. Did he know he was dying, and was this the reason for offering the business for sale, and then making himself voluntarily bankrupt to protect the assets of other members of the family? If so, why is there no record of his death, either in parish registers or in the press? Was the business actually failing and did the shame of this drive John to suicide, which might explain the lack of death records? Whatever the situation, it was left to his two sons, Thomas and Robert, to pick up the pieces.

Chapter 2

The Business expands, and
the *Pegasus* is built

At the time of John's death, Thomas, the elder son, was twenty-four, and a partner in the firm of Barclay and Skirving, Auctioneers and Appraisers, with premises in Glasgow's Trongate, one of the major streets of the city at that time. Robert was twenty-two and the one who had been actively involved in the Shipwright business. Both men continued to live in what had been their father's house.

Immediately after John's death, Robert was recorded in the *Post Office Directory* as a 'Shipwright, Stobcross Slip', but with the note that orders would be received at Barclay and Skirving. The brothers were working together to try to salvage the business. The Receiver seems to have abandoned attempts to sell the Stobcross Yard. In 1828 there are further signs of the Company's recovery. There was an application for John's Bankruptcy to be discharged and the new directory entry for the business is:

Barclay, Robert, & Co. shipwrights, Stobcross Slip, Finnieston, and 31, McAlpine Street.

Robert had found a partner, and from other sources, 31 McAlpine Street can be identified as a Blacksmith's Shop, doubtless producing the necessary metalwork for the ships under construction or repair. There must have been an injection of money into the business from somewhere. A public auction or roup was held in January for the Liverpool registered brig *Kitty,* which had been left on the Stobcross Slip, the sale presumably to recover the unpaid costs of repairs. Additional money almost certainly came from Thomas (or he raised it from some of his associates). Although there is no explicit record of a partnership being set up between Robert and Thomas, from that time until 1840, when there is a record of Thomas withdrawing from the Partnership on 20 January; both men appear to have been actively involved in the Stobcross business. Until 1830/31 the brothers also continue to share their father's house in York Street. By 1831, Robert had moved into a house on what was then called Steam Boat Quay, but shortly after was renamed Anderston Quay; more or less 'living above the shop'. Thomas settled himself in the city, changing houses every two or three years, probably being upwardly mobile as we would say today, but at this distance in time, it is difficult to be sure.

In 1832, there are the first records of Robert Barclay & Co. building rather than repairing ships. The first was the *Glasgow Merchant* – a two masted schooner. The brothers are recorded as the first owners, so possibly it was a speculative build with a view to selling the completed ship. Although there are no further records for this ship, the enterprise must have been successful as the Company then built and launched a further three ships in the same year – two wooden paddle steamers, the *Inverness* for Messrs Young, Smith Melvin & Turner, and the *Staffa* for the Staffa Steam Boat Company, both intended for coastal trade, but more significantly the *Lusitania,* a brigantine for the Glasgow merchant John Mitchell to use in the cork trade with Portugal. The *Morning Post* reported that this was the first sea-going vessel to be built in Glasgow, and that its launch attracted a great number of spectators. This was the good publicity that Robert Barclay & Co. needed. Mitchell was certainly satisfied with his purchase as in 1835 he took delivery of the schooner *Lisbon* from them for the same route.

Over the next three years, records show that Barclay & Co. built a further three coastal paddle steamers, a paddle tug, and two three-masted barques, one for a Liverpool company. Of particular interest to the story of the *Pegasus,* was one of the steam paddle-boats, the *Northern Yacht*, launched in May 1835 and built for the Barclays themselves to operate on the Glasgow to Millport run. Subsequently Thomas took sole ownership and transferred the ship to a route between Newhaven, Edinburgh and Dundee, before selling it on to the Shields and Newcastle Steam Navigation Company, for use on a route between Hull, Newcastle and Leith. Shortly after the sale, the *Northern Yacht* came to grief on the Farne Islands.

By the middle of the 1830s, the Company had established itself as successful shipbuilders, building a variety of different vessels, but they were also starting to dabble in using their own ships commercially. It seems likely that Thomas was the driving force behind this move, probably both as a means of earning the company extra money and developing an aspect of the business in which he, as a businessman, could be more directly involved. These initiatives highlighted for him the so far unrealised potential for East Coast shipping routes.

These strands came together in 1835, when the brothers decided to build the paddle steamer *Pegasus* and use it to provide a twice weekly service between Hull and Leith. Although to modern eyes it does not seem a particularly exciting route, in those days it was potentially a very lucrative one. The 'new-fangled' railways were still only just getting under way. Although Liverpool and Manchester had been connected in 1830, followed by a line between Manchester and Birmingham, so far they had had no impact on East Coast travel. A fine steamer completing the journey between Hull and Leith in twenty-four hours was a far more attractive prospect than at least two days bumping north in a coach. The Government had need of an efficient means of moving the mail to North Britain, as they labelled it, and also for the swift transport of soldiers to serve in the northern garrisons at Inverness, Perth, Edinburgh and Berwick.

Barclay and Curle's Slip Dock, 1845 by William Simpson
000-000-131-571-C — ©*Glasgow Museums*

Most important of all, was that Birmingham and the surrounding towns increasingly became the workshop of Britain, if not the world. With the aid of a canal link to Hull, the route offered excellent transport links for the Scottish markets; nor was it all one-way trade – after years of droving cattle to the south for the growing towns, the animals could now complete half the journey in a day with little loss of weight. Grain, coal, whisky and iron were also likely cargoes. It was doubtless with these considerations in mind, that, in setting up the infrastructure for their Leith/Hull route, the Barclays did not employ one of Hull's established shipping agents. Instead, they went into business with John Thompson & Co. (later Thompson McKay). John Thompson had begun his career as a canal broker in Manchester at the start of the nineteenth century. He based himself at Rochdale Canal Wharf, the Manchester end of the canal route through to Hull, and developed his business to become a carrier on the rapidly expanding canal network. By 1835 the company he founded could be described as 'the Canal's leading public carrier, paying £5,528 in tolls -10% of the total Rochdale canal toll income'.[1]

It was a shrewd move, ensuring that the Company was well positioned to benefit from the ever-growing trade from the Midlands and the North West.

The ship the Barclays planned was to be 'state of the art'. She was a hybrid, equipped with engines made by one of the most noted Scottish manufacturers, Tod & Macgregor, but also schooner rigged. The combination was designed for economical operation – no need to use the engines if the winds were good, but also to ensure that the advertised service was not disrupted by unfavourable weather. The *Pegasus* was large – 132 feet four inches long, 18½ feet wide (39 feet across the paddle boxes) and, having consideration for her proposed cargo carrying role, a deep hold

---

1 Maw, Wyke & Kidd: Journal of Transport History 3/2 Dec. 2009

of 11 feet one inch. To meet the needs of her passengers she was luxuriously appointed with fixtures and fittings of 'the very best quality and elegance'. The main sleeping cabins were panelled in mahogany; there were also four lavishly furnished family state rooms under the quarter deck at the stern. Copper-bottoming would help maintain her speed.

The new ship was formally registered in Glasgow on 13 December 1835, with the owners listed as the Hull and Leith Steam Packet Company (HLSPC) of Leith. The shareholders of the new company were Thomas and Robert Barclay, also Robert Cook, who had been appointed master of the new vessel. On 30 September 1836, Robert Cook married Janet Barclay, the brothers' younger sister, so, in dividing the shareholding with the captain of their new flagship, the brothers were certainly giving him encouragement to do his best for the enterprise, but possibly with the assurance that the money would be kept within the family. It is worth noting that the *Pegasus* joined the British merchant fleet at a time when less than 5% of registered shipping was steam powered, and most of those ships were river craft.

The *Pegasus* was launched on or about 20 January 1836, and proceeded to complete her trials on 21 January, taking two hours to sail to Gourock against a strong breeze, and in competition with one of the fastest of the river boats. It was all very successful – according to the *Glasgow Courier* – 'the result established *Pegasus* as a sailor of the very first class'.

By now, the new service was being widely advertised in newspapers across Britain with notices in, among others, the Hull, London, Staffordshire and Manchester papers.

STEAM CONVEYANCE BETWEEN HULL AND LEITH,
CALLING OFF SCARBOROUGH, WHITBY, &c.
THE powerful and splendid new Steam-Ship, PEGASUS, captain ROBERT COOK, built expressly for the Hull and Leith

Trade, will be on the Station in a week or two, her Machinery being already fitted up. Her Accommodations for Passengers are of the most commodious and elegant description, comprising every comfort of which any Steamer can boast. Besides large Sleeping Cabins for Ladies and for Gentlemen, she has Four distinct State-Rooms, in each of which a small Party or Family can be accommodated.

The great dimensions of this Vessel secure ample Stowage for Goods, and the average time of her trips between Hull and Leith will not exceed Twenty-Four Hours.

Hull Packet 1 January 1836

Fares were given in subsequent advertisements – twenty-five shillings for the cabin (with two shillings to the steward); 12/6 steerage, and freight charges – sixpence per foot. She had also secured a valuable mail contract with the Post Office – this was a definite asset – mail was a high value cargo, but one which occupied small space on the ship. Those sending letters by the *Pegasus* had to mark them *per Pegasus Steamer*, and deliver them to the post office an hour before sailing.

All that remained was to get the *Pegasus* to her station at Leith. Small ships used the Forth and Clyde canal to cross from west to east, and the majority of the remainder sailed through the Great Glen on Telford's Caledonian Canal, reaching the East Coast at Inverness, thus avoiding the dangers of the Pentland Firth. The *Pegasus*, however, was too large for either of those routes and so had to take the longest and most dangerous passage round the north of Scotland, at the worst time of year.

Nor was the weather good for the voyage – the whole of Britain had experienced what the newspapers generally described as a hurricane moving north in the last days of January. It certainly caused considerable damage across the country. The *Pegasus* probably encountered the tail end of this as she entered the Pentland Firth, but she proved more than capable of handling the conditions. On

10 February 1836, *The Scotsman* reported her arrival at Leith on Saturday 6 February at four o'clock, with the following comments:

> The passage round the north ... served one purpose effectually – the proving her capabilities as a seaboat in the hardest weather that blows. So stormy a period as that which she has just weathered is of rare occurrence; and her speed and power have been most satisfactorily demonstrated.

It was an auspicious beginning.

CHAPTER 3

THE *PEGASUS* ENTERS SERVICE

No time was wasted on fine adjustments for the *Pegasus* after her rough journey from Glasgow. The next day she entered service, beginning her first commercial voyage to Hull on the afternoon of Sunday 7 February. Again, she encountered stormy weather, and rather than the advertised twenty-four hours, it took thirty to reach Hull. There, however, she received a warm welcome, and before sailing back to Leith, there was time for visitors to look over the ship's facilities. The local newspaper, *The Hull Packet* gave strong support to the enterprise:

> ... after attracting a great number of visitors, who appeared highly delighted with her elegance, she sailed for Leith on Wednesday morning, and went down the river in gallant style. Such a conveyance has been long wanted, and we have no doubt that the spirited undertaking will meet with abundant success.
>
> *Hull Packet* 12 February 1836

More positive publicity followed the *Pegasus'* second sailing to Hull. On this occasion, as she reached Bridlington, she met with the whaling ship *Abram*, which, along with much of the Hull whaling fleet, had been trapped by ice in the Davis Straits throughout the winter. Six ships had been totally lost, and now the *Abram*, having broken free of the ice on 30 January, was returning home, bringing with her survivors from three of the sunken ships – the *Dordon*, the *Lee* and the *Mary Frances*. As the faster ship, the *Pegasus* agreed to take on board the captains and surgeons of the *Dordon* and the *Mary Frances*, and two unnamed seamen. They reached Hull on 14 February, two days ahead of the *Abram*, bringing definite news of the whaling fleet's fate. Although it was not all good news, there was great relief in the town, that at last they knew what had happened. The rescue had owed little to the *Pegasus*, but nevertheless she featured in all reports of it, and was present during the rejoicing which followed the men's return, doubtless being one of the ships which hoisted her colours to the peals of church bells.

Gradually, the Company's sailings fell into a fixed schedule, leaving Leith on a Saturday afternoon and returning from Hull on a Wednesday, where, because of the tidal access, exact times of departure varied from week to week. It was not until 2 July 1836, that the *Pegasus* almost achieved the published time of twenty-four hours for her voyage. Leaving Leith at two-thirty p.m. and calling at both Whitby and Scarborough on the way, she docked at Hull at three p.m. the following day. Certainly, it was proving a popular route – a report of the voyage a fortnight later includes the information that the ship carried 'upwards of ninety passengers'.

The Company, however, did not have it all its own way. It faced competition from the much longer established Irish St. George's Steam Packet Company. Founded in 1821, the Irish company had run routes serving Liverpool, the Isle of Man, North Wales and Bristol and in 1831, even sent the paddle steamer *Sophia Jane* to Australia! In 1834, they established a base at Hull to serve seasonal routes to Gothenburg, Hamburg and Rotterdam. In 1836, at about the same time as the *Pegasus* entered service on the Leith/Hull route, they introduced sailings on the same route. These were to continue until about 1840. In Spring 1836, their flagship, the *St. George,* was advertised as providing a better and cheaper service – it had two 55 horsepower engines, as opposed to the *Pegasus'* single one, and it offered first class tickets for five shillings, and second class for three shillings. These were not claims which *could be allowed* to go unchallenged. In July 1836, the Company published the following statement regarding the *Pegasus*:

The Pegasus has proved her decided superiority in the severest Weather on her present station; and Puffs to her disadvantage come with a bad grace from a Vessel which *has been regularly beat here and elsewhere*, and has now only SECOND-HAND ENGINES, saved from the wreck of another boat. Accidents from OLD ENGINES are tenfold more numerous than from those of the Pegasus' construction, and most frequently arise from DEFICIENT BOILERS. The Pegasus has TWO which are NEW and UNSCORCHED.

Hull Advertiser and Exchange Gazette 22 July 1836

The war of words with the *St. George Steam Packet Company* was to continue for the rest of the year. On 4 November, another notice appeared in the press:

THE PEGASUS, – This splendid steam-ship still continues to ply between this port and Leith with her accustomed regularity. During the heavy weather of last week, which has proved so fatal to shipping, she made her passage down against a tremendous head wind all the way. After discharging and loading, she again left Leith on Saturday evening, and arrived here on Sunday about nine P.M., having met about noon that day, while off Scarborough, the St. George, which had sailed with her the previous Wednesday, still on her passage to Leith.

Hull Advertiser and Exchange Gazette

The *St. George* and its sister ship the *Innisfail* continued to challenge the Company's monopoly of the Hull/Leith route until the end of the decade, but then the Irish company, its resources overstretched, reduced its continental services and seems to have abandoned the coastal route to Leith, Dundee and Aberdeen.

The HLSPC, however, was not problem free during 1836. The *Pegasus* encountered its first serious difficulty in August 1836. Setting sail from Leith on 6 August, in the words of *The Hull Packet*, it 'struck on a sunken rock nearly opposite Bamborough

Castle. She arrived safe on Tuesday last'. The incident was also reported in *The Scotsman* of 10 August:

> The Pegasus steamer, on her passage from Leith to Hull, went on shore on the Ferne Islands, about seven o'clock on the evening of Saturday last. The passengers and crew were, however, with the aid of boats from the Northumberland coast, safely landed; and we are happy in being enabled to state, that the Pegasus was so little damaged that she proceeded on to Hull with her goods and passengers, on Monday at 12 o'clock, from Newton Haven Bay, on the coast of Northumberland.

There is no mention of this incident in the surviving Barclays' records, but it is referred to in two letters published by *The Times* after the sinking of the *Pegasus*, and one of the passengers, Robert Skeen, a London printer, returning home after visiting his family in Tweedmouth, included an account of the events in a privately published autobiography. He recorded that he was chatting to other passengers on deck, when just after they passed the Farne Islands, the ship struck an underwater rock with such force that several people were knocked to the ground. The ship's bows were pierced, and five feet of water entered the hold. The *Pegasus* raised a distress signal, which brought help from a fishing boat, whose master skilfully ran the steamer ashore between two ledges of rock.

The passengers disembarked to find themselves at the small village of Newton-by-the-Sea, where they were left to their own devices. Skeen and some of the others walked in the direction of Dunstanburgh Castle, admiring the scenery. Meanwhile Captain Cook returned to Edinburgh to report the accident, and to make arrangements for repair. He brought back several carpenters, who worked on the ship during the low tides. It was fit to sail again on the Monday, although Skeen said that a number of the passengers, not surprisingly, preferred to complete the journey by road. His comments on the cause of the accident, however, are particularly interesting:

It (*the rock*) was not marked in the chart – but there are many such on that coast – and the captain ought to have kept further out. His silly excuse was that he wished the passengers to have a good view of the picturesque and precipitous shores of Northumberland!

One of the letters to *The Times* suggested another cause for the accident. The author, who used the initials W.W. and wrote from Bedford, explained that because of the damage to the *Pegasus*, in 1836, he had had to travel north on the *St. George*, and on the voyage had asked one of her officers the reason for the accident to the *Pegasus*. He was told that, 'it was entirely owing to her going too near the shore in attempting to get before the *St. George*; and that not long before she was nearly wrecked on the mud at the mouth of the Humber from the same cause'. Although both these accounts suggest that Captain Cook's judgement was at fault, Oxoniensis, the writer of the other letter to *The Times*, stated that many of the passengers signed a testimonial to the effect that the Captain was not to blame.

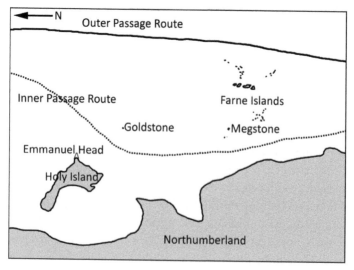

Alternative sailing routes along the north Northumberland coast.

Some seven weeks later, the Captain, Robert Cook, married the Barclays' sister, Janet, – so, whatever Skeen's opinion, presumably the brothers did not find Cook culpable for the accident to their ship. Perhaps they should have done. Ships sailing along the North East coast of England had two options when they drew near the Farne Islands – they could either go further out to sea by-passing the Islands and their associated rocks on the landward side, or they could choose the shorter and quicker so-called Inner Passage, said to be perfectly safe, provided the appropriate channel markers were kept carefully aligned. Nevertheless, it was generally regarded as a riskier route, susceptible to changes in tide and wind.

After the problems of August 1836, the *Pegasus* resumed her regular routes with no incidents of note for the rest of the year. At the beginning of 1837 she was withdrawn briefly from service for maintenance work to both paddles and machinery. When the ship came back on station in March 1837, it was with the claim that the work 'will much accelerate her speed'. Passenger accommodation seems to have been improved at the same time, as advertisements from this date refer to six rather than the earlier four state rooms. Perhaps as a result of competition from the *St. George*, prices were also lowered. The best cabin was now eighteen shillings, with two shillings for the steward; goods were from ten shillings to £1 per ton and light goods fourpence a foot. Despite reducing costs, the company was clearly doing well – a second ship, the *Ardencaple* was added to the Leith/Hull run, probably in May 1837.

Travelling on the *Pegasus* in 1837 is described in a letter by 'C' to the Editor of *The Scotsman*, dated May 26, shortly after the refit.

We sailed in the *Pegasus* from Leith for Hull, on Saturday the 20th of May, at half-past three, P.M. The east wind had blown for many days and raised a heavy swell, which was increased by the wind rising to a gale at midnight. It was directly in our favour, and, between steam and wind, we landed safely at Hull, at half-past four, P.M. on Sunday. The *Pegasus* is not large, but sails well; and although her sleeping cabins are cribs, and sadly crowded, her captain is attentive, her cookery good, and the ladies reported that she has an admirable stewardess, full of spontaneous kindness and never-tiring activity. (*published 17 June 1837*).

Perhaps the increase in the number of staterooms had been at the expense of the spaciousness so praised when she first entered service.

In September 1837, another *Pegasus* advertisement sniped at a rival vessel (presumably the *St. George*):

> The PEGASUS being built expressly for the *station*, has the satisfactory advantage of being able to land her passengers on her *arrival*, thereby superseding the disagreeable necessity of landing them in *Small Boats*.
>
> *Caledonian Mercury* 28 September 1837

It is not clear where or to what exactly this refers, but possibly it was the access to the Hull Inner Dock, which could only be reached by sailing up the Humber at high tide.

Generally, 1837 was uneventful, as were the early months of 1838. An advertisement in the *Caledonian Mercury*, provides the first indication of cargo carried by the *Pegasus*.

> WILLIAM ADAMS respectfully informs his numerous Customers and the Public, that he leaves this day per Pegasus Steamer, for Worcester, Staffordshire, and the Glass Manufacturing districts of England, and that to enable him to make room for his intended purchases, he has resolved to continue the CHEAP SALE FOR ONE WEEK LONGER. ....
> New Worcester Royal Porcelain and Flint Glass Show Rooms, Sign of the Gilded Tureen,
> 42, SOUTH BRIDGE, EDINBURGH
>
> July 28, 1838

Certainly, the expensive crockery and glass being purchased by Mr Adams, would be less likely to be broken in the ship's hold than on wagons travelling over rough roads.

In September 1838, came an event which must have given all the east coast shipping companies pause for thought – the Hull/Dundee packet, the *Forfarshire*, hampered by damaged boilers, and relying solely on her sails, sank off the Farne Islands in a storm on Thursday 6 September, with the loss of forty-three passengers and crew. There were only eighteen survivors, half of them famously rescued by Grace Darling and her father, rowing out from the Longstone Lighthouse. Surprisingly, an account of how events unfolded on that last voyage survives, written by a passenger aboard the *Pegasus:*

> We left Hull by the *Pegasus* on Wednesday last, in company with the *Innisfail*[2] and the ill-fated *Forfarshire*. The latter was laid alongside the *Pegasus* in the Humber dock, from which we sailed, and appeared to be a large and well-fitted steamer. I could not help contrasting her with our own ship, and wishing that we had had the advantage of her larger size and double engine, little thinking that the race would soon be given to the weaker. The *Forfarshire* took the lead, and passed the Pier Head at twenty minutes past six o' clock: in ten minutes more we followed her, and the *Innisfail* at a similar interval followed us.
> The lead was kept by the *Forfarshire* for a mile or two down the Humber, when she crossed our bows, and after running parallel with us for a short time, began to lose way, so that before we reached the Spurn, her light was seen at least a mile astern of us … it was evident something was *then* going wrong … Owing to the thick state of the weather (as we supposed) we saw nothing more of the *Forfarshire* …
>
> *Leeds Mercury* 15 September 1838

---

2 This was the St. George's Steam Packet ship

Following the accident, a discussion about the wisdom of the *Forfarshire* using the Inner Passage, includes the specific statement that this was the route the *Pegasus* had used on that voyage. Clearly the events off Bamburgh in 1836, had not caused Captain Cook to change his navigation route.

The *Pegasus* had been lucky on that occasion, but, on Sunday, 16 December 1838, when sailing from Leith to Hull, at six a.m. she went aground on the Salt Scar Rocks off Redcar in the fog. Fortunately, the ship was only a mile from land; boats came out from Redcar and many of the passengers disembarked to continue their journey by other means. The ship was floated off the rocks on the rising tide and made for Hartlepool, where she underwent repairs before continuing to Hull. Captain Cook does not seem to have been blamed for this incident. The Salt Scar Rocks were notorious – that year alone eleven ships had foundered on them – and in the fog, precise steering was impossible. Moreover, once he had struck the rocks, he had handled the situation well, enabling the passengers to land, successfully refloating the ship, and getting it to a port for repair.

If, on Hogmanay, as Scots often do, Robert Cook reviewed the year that had passed, he must have reflected that he had had two lucky escapes. Would his luck hold in the year ahead?

CHAPTER 4

FOUNDERED AT ST. MONANS

At the beginning of 1839, Robert Cook's career took a different turn, for he seems to have moved temporarily from captaining the *Pegasus*, to undertaking office duties in Leith for the Company.

As had become the custom, the *Pegasus* was withdrawn from service for a major overhaul in January 1839. She had only just returned to service in the middle of February, when she once more attracted attention for her part in a sea rescue. This time, the ship in trouble was the schooner *Anna* of Weymouth, carrying a cargo of grain from London to Leith. She was struck by a heavy squall off the island of Inchkeith in the Firth of Forth. The ship heeled over, and with this, the cargo of grain shifted in the hold, preventing the ship righting herself. She began to sink almost immediately and was under the waves within ten minutes. When the squall struck, the *Pegasus* had been about a mile away, but using all her steam power, she was able to get alongside very quickly. Lowering the ship's boat, her crew rescued two of the sailors who had jumped into the water and brought them safely on board the ship. Sadly, both the *Anna's* master and the cabin boy got caught up in the wreckage and drowned.

Two months later there was a reverse of fortunes. On 1 May, at about seven p.m., the *Pegasus* left Hull for the voyage to Leith. She was laden with what was described as a 'general' cargo, and, according to the captain's sworn statement, carried between forty and fifty passengers. (It was customary to keep a record of those passengers who had booked tickets for the voyage, but there were always others who arrived on the day, and of them no record was kept. Newspaper accounts of the event which followed gave the number of passengers as between ninety and a hundred). When the ship left the Humber, the weather was clear and winds moderate, but as they sailed north, the visibility worsened. By eight p.m. the following evening, when the ship was off the coast between Berwick and Eyemouth, the fog was so bad that no land could be seen. The captain, now a Neil Cook, ordered the engines to half-speed, and began regular depth soundings, one of the sailors paying out a lead weighted rope to check the depth of the water. By this means at nine p.m. he recorded a depth of 35 fathoms; continuing at half speed, at midnight he recorded 25 fathoms. He had no way of judging exactly where he was, however, and by maintaining the compass bearing which had brought them up the coast, they had sailed directly across the Firth of Forth, missing the turn along the south bank of the river to reach Leith and, at about one o'clock on the Friday morning, struck a rock on the Fife coast, halfway between Elie and St. Monans.

The captain's first effort was to try and refloat the ship. Using the engines, he succeeded after half an hour, but it immediately became apparent that there was serious damage to the hull, and the ship was leaking badly. According to the newspaper accounts, within a few minutes, water was knee-high in the engine room. Urgent action was needed if passengers, cargo and ship were to be saved. Fortunately, a passing fisherman, having heard the crash, came to see what had happened. With his help, and before the engine room was totally flooded, Cook was able to run the ship aground on the adjacent shore. It was now about two a.m. The ship secure, orders were given to raise the alarm. The ship's bell was rung, and guns fired. The noise woke the neighbourhood, and more boats came out from St. Monans and took the passengers safely ashore.

That we know so much about the events of that night is due to the sworn statements which the captain, together with the second mate and the engineer, gave to the notary public at Anstruther, over the next two days. These were designed to clear the captain and crew from responsibility for the accident, and to demonstrate that they had used *every exertion in their power for the safety and preserving of the said ship and cargo.* If these statements were accepted, the insurers and those who consigned the goods to the ship, would have to bear at least some of the costs and losses incurred.

After securing the ship and landing the passengers, the next priority was as far as possible to secure the cargo. Cargo details, drawn from the salvage documents prepared after the accident, are given in the next chapter, but in general terms, it included foodstuffs, agricultural items, tools, metal goods, fabric and wool, oil, and household necessities such as soap. Some 150 companies or individuals had consigned goods on the *Pegasus*. Mixed with these items were the personal belongings of individual passengers. Cook began organising the cargo's discharge and storage at St. Monans and the neighbouring village of Elie. Cellars and warehousing were rented, and over twenty local men employed, at fees ranging from £2.5s.0d to £5.16s.4d, to get the cargo from the ship to safe storage. Constables were hired to guard the cargo in its temporary storage. Thanks to Cook's prompt action, according to the records, all the cargo was rescued with the exception of 'some seed &c of trifling value'.

Cook then turned his attention to his own and his crew's welfare. He needed to find accommodation for the sailors until such time as the *Pegasus* could be refloated. Mrs Janet Brown in St. Monans provided board and lodging for some of the men at a cost of £7.6s.0d for five days. The rest were lodged with Mrs Ovenston at the *Ship Inn* in Elie, together with carpenters sent over to help with the repairs, at a total cost of £11.17s.0d.

Lastly, Cook needed to protect both his crew and himself from blame for what, as they saw it, had been an unavoidable accident occasioned by the weather. This was a two-stage process, according to the custom of the day. Firstly, Neil Cook went to the mast of the *Pegasus*, gathered his crew there, and then formally protested:

that he and they should be free of all damage sustained or to
be sustained by the said Vessel and Cargo, the same not having
been occasioned by any insufficiency of his said Vessel or fault
to neglect of him or his Crew, but entirely owing to the dense
fog and thickness of the weather ...

University of Glasgow Library, Archives & Special
Collections UGD 255/4/35/2

Having made his protest before his crew, he then left the ship and
made his way to the neighbouring town of Anstruther where he
found Matthew Foster Connolly. Connolly was the town clerk
there, but more importantly from Cook's point of view, he was
the notary public – the official licensed to take and record oaths.
There, in front of local witnesses, Cook repeated the oath he had
made to his crew on board the ship, which was duly recorded by
Connolly. The following day, William Hall, the second mate of
the *Pegasus*, and James French, the ship's engineer had to go to
Anstruther and swear to the truth of Cook's declaration. This
too was duly witnessed and recorded.

With the legal niceties completed, the Company's attention now
turned to getting the *Pegasus* repaired and the goods back to Leith.
Both Robert Barclay, the ship's builder, and Robert Cook, the
former captain, came to Elie to supervise proceedings. Moving
the cargo was a significant undertaking. Two ships were hired to
carry the goods back to Leith – the *Queen of Scotts* and the *Dainty
Davie*. Fife coopers were also hired to replace or repair barrel con-
tainers which had been damaged when the ship had struck the
rocks. Other costs involved in getting things put right included
the legal expenses, new ropes, the printing of notices informing
the customers what was happening, and renting warehouse space
in Leith until the goods and their recipients could be re-united.

Cook's version of events in his oath was accepted. It followed that,
as the accident was not the fault of the Steam Packet Company
or its agents, they could not be held solely liable for damage to

goods. As a result, the consigners of the goods, shipping agents, companies or private owners, accepted a shared liability for the average loss to ship and cargo. That would be allocated according to the value of the various goods in the cargo. David Thom, a Leith merchant, was appointed the arbiter for these proceedings, and published his schedule of awards on 24 September 1839. He found that the Company was liable for £582.9s.9d; while those that had consigned cargo were liable for their proportions of £240.11s.6d. This settlement seems to have been accepted without dispute.

Moving the ship was done in two stages; firstly, it was refloated, using empty barrels and oil casks as additional floats, and then towed to Elie Harbour by the steamer *George*. Presumably, temporary repairs were carried out there by the carpenters brought over from Leith. Then the ship was moved on to Dundee, where the work was completed at Thomas Adamson's shipbuilding yard on the Tay. A Peter Horne was employed to oversee the repairs to the engine. Once both were fully repaired, Lloyd's surveyors from both Dundee and Leith certified that the *Pegasus* was fit to resume sailing, on 16 May 1839, as advertised in the *Leeds Mercury* of 25 May 1839:

HULL AND LEITH.

THE SPLENDID STEAMSHIP *PEGASUS* will resume the above Station on *Saturday first*, and is appointed to leave HULL for LEITH every WEDNESDAY as usual, at the following Hours–

29th May at 5 o'Clock P.M.   12th June at 5 P.M.

5th June at 10 P.M.   19th June at 10 A.M.

Returning from Leith every SATURDAY, and making the Passage in little more than 24 Hours.

Best Cabin Fare 20s.; Second Do. 7s. 6d.

Goods for this Conveyance should be down the Day before sailing, specially addressed to the care of the Agents.

THOMPSON, McKAY & CO.

8, Pier Street, Hull.

The Damage recently sustained by the PEGASUS having been substantially repaired, at Dundee, under the Direction and to the Satisfaction of Lloyds' Surveyors for Leith and Dundee; we, the undersigned, hereby certify, that the Hull and Machinery of the PEGASUS are in the highest State of Efficiency and Repair.

> WALTER PATEN, Lloyds' Surveyor at Leith.
> D. CRIGHTEN, Lloyds' Surveyor at Dundee.
> THOS. ADAMSON, Ship Builder, Dundee.
> PETER BODDIE, Engineer, Dundee.
>
> Dundee, 16th May, 1839.

Despite all his efforts to clear himself, Neil Cook seems to have been blamed by the Company for the accident. Certainly, by October 1839, there was a new master on the *Pegasus* – a John Brown. Brown was a Stirlingshire man, who, before being appointed to the *Pegasus*, had captained the *Benledi*, a Barclay built and owned iron steamer, sailing daily between Edinburgh and Stirling, and serving the Firth of Forth Ports. So, the Company already knew the skills of the man being appointed. He was certainly an experienced captain. When he was elected a vice president of the International Shipwreck Society in the following year, the honour was duly reported in *The Hull Packet* of 7 August 1840, with the comment that the honour had been 'justly conferred, as Captain Brown has been the means of saving many persons from a watery grave'.

Less easily measured was damage done to the reputation of the *Pegasus*. Until May 1839, the Company had been very successful in minimising any problems the *Pegasus* had had, but the accident on the Fife coast was different – it made news in papers across the country – in Whitby, the *Pegasus* was described as *'wrecked'* while the *Yorkshire Gazette* stated that she was *'lost'*. In a competitive market, the gloss which until now had attached itself to the *Pegasus* name since her launch in 1836, was well and truly tarnished.

CHAPTER 5

CARGO

Although a misfortune for the HLSPC, for the historian, the accident at St. Monans provides a unique insight into the cargo carried by the *Pegasus,* the businesses which used her, and aspects of the society she served. No bills of lading survive, and the only extant accounts for the ship, which have been found, are bills for coal to fuel the engines. The need to deal with the insurance issues arising from the accident, however, meant that in May/June 1839, a 'Statement of Salvage Charges' was prepared. This gives a list of the goods being shipped and names of those to whom they were being sent. In all, 152 consignees were listed; at this distance in time, some must remain obscure – a W. Robertson, the intended recipient of two Boxes, is unidentifiable, as is D. Travers whose carpet bag is listed, and A. Dunsmure who had a parcel on board. Indeed these, and some others, may simply have been passengers on board, and the items listed their personal luggage. Interspersed with these unknowns, however, are those who were and, in some instances still are, significant enterprises. The largest of all was the British Army, but identifiable industrialists and shopkeepers also feature. Accompanying the names, are short descriptions of the items carried. In some instances, the descriptions are also uninformative – 'a hamper', 'a box', 'a truss', mean very little; 'butter', 'yarn', 'leather', 'scythes' on the other hand give a sense of the variety of cargo. When matched against the names of some consignees, they can also throw light on the way the shipping line contributed to Scottish trade and industry, and the significance of the sea route linking Yorkshire and the Midlands through Hull to Leith.

The Company held a government contract to convey army equipment and personnel transferring to Scottish barracks from ones in England or overseas, and vice versa. This facilitated rapid movement of troops if need arose, as travel warrants could be issued immediately by the army, and would be honoured by the Company whenever the troops and equipment arrived at the docks. As far as the *Pegasus* was concerned, she was used mainly for the transportation of troops to and from the Scottish barracks at Edinburgh, Stirling, Perth and Dundee. Those stations further north, or on the west coast, were served by other shipping routes. The records show that in May 1839, she was carrying baggage whose salvage worth was £230 – the largest single payment made – for the 3rd Dragoon Guards, who were moving from their station at Norwich to Piershill Barracks in Edinburgh, together with a horse and carriage belonging to John Daniel Dyson, one of their captains. It is possible that the horse was Dyson's bay gelding, *Dust,* which the 1839 *Racing Calendar* shows him racing later that year at Musselburgh. Almost certainly a contingent of the 3rd Dragoon Guards, though not listed, were among the passengers.

With the proximity of the cloth mills of the West Riding to Hull, it is not surprising that cloth of one type or another formed a significant proportion of the cargo. In all, thirty-one trusses of fabric are listed for fourteen different consignees. We know from the sale of shipwrecked cargo from the *Pegasus,* held at Leith on 17 May 1839, that among the fabrics were: 600 yards of superfine broadcloth; cassimeres (these were also known as *kerseymere* and were fine-twilled woollen cloths of worsted warp and woollen weft, in a diagonal twill weave, used to make lightweight men's suits); and pilot cloths (a heavy twilled woollen overcoating with a thick nap used especially for seamen's blue uniforms). The largest customer was J. Clapperton & Co., Woollen Merchants, in Edinburgh's High Street, who, in mid-May, advertised new stocks of black cloth, saxony wool, kerseys, cassimeres and dowskin. Were they among the cargo items successfully rescued at St. Monans? Another notable customer was A. Thompson & Co., Wholesale and Retail Woollen Drapers, also in the High Street, who was due four trusses. Among the other consignees was the recently formed company of Kennington and Jenner, Silk Mercers, Linen Drapers & Haberdashers, in Princes Street, now Edinburgh's famous department store, Jenners, still on its original site. These and several other consignees were basically textile retailers. Others required the materials for the manufacture of garments. Peter Scott on South Bridge was not only a draper but also a clothier and shirt merchant; Pantons & McIntosh in Bank Street were clothiers, and J. Christie and Sons of George Street were breeches makers. Apart from highlighting the range of natural fabrics in regular use, the identification of the different merchants and their addresses is one of the first indications of Edinburgh's shift in gravity from the Old Town's High Street, by way of South Bridge, to the more fashionable New Town; Princes Street and George Street, developing to the north of the recently created Princes Street Gardens.

FABRICS FROM THE *PEGASUS*

FABRIC	TYPE OF FABRIC	USE
Superfine Broadcloth	A plain-woven wool cloth which was then shrunk to produce dense weatherproof finish	Men's suiting
Cassimere/ Kerseymere	Lightweight twilled woollen fabric	Lightweight suiting
Pilot Cloth	Heavyweight wool overcoating with a thick nap	Seamen's Uniforms
Kersey	A thick sturdy woven cloth	Military uniforms and greatcoats
Dowskin/ Doeskin	A lustrous tightly woven water-resistant wool cloth	Female clothing, particularly where draping is required
Saxon Wool	A fine merino wool woven fabric	Dresses, suits and scarves

A different use for wool was developed by Richard Whytock & Co. This company was established as furniture warehousemen in George Street in 1807, but by the 1830s, had diversified into carpet manufacturers, patenting a *Tapestry Carpet Loom* in 1832. They converted a disused distillery at Lasswade into a factory producing hand knotted carpets in the Turkish and Persian style. In 1838, the company received a Royal Warrant from Queen Victoria. The truss consigned to Whytock on the *Pegasus* probably contained carpet wool.

Heavy goods from the Midlands were brought to Hull by canal before being sent on as sea cargo to Scotland. Five ironmongers and an iron merchant were the intended recipients of such goods on the *Pegasus*. J. Sibbald & Sons of George Street, retailers of, among other things, kitchen ranges and patent coffee pots, were consigned '3 fronts & 1 box'. Were the 'fronts' replacement doors for the kitchen ranges? Russell & Clark, ironmongers in Hunter Square had ordered fifteen bundles of scythes and a bag of nails; Drummond & Son of Stirling were due six bundles of scythes; Laird and Hampton of Leith expected six bags of nails, and D. Watson ironmonger in the High Street had ordered a bundle of saws. There were three separate consignments of steel, the largest of which, seven bundles was for R. Laidlaw & Co., Brassfounders and Bellhangers, with businesses in both Edinburgh and Glasgow. Glass and china followed the same route from the Midlands, and were sent for J. & W. Bailey, china dealers in the Candlemarket, and William Adams, whose glass and china warehouse was on South Bridge.

Another bulky cargo was pipes of oil. The type of oil is never specified but was most likely whale oil brought into Hull by the Arctic whalers. At the time of the grounding, the *Pegasus* was carrying six pipes of oil, each pipe holding approximately 475 litres. Two of the pipes went separately to Edinburgh firms of paint manufacturers – William Dawson of Elbe Street and William Young of Bonington Road. The remaining four were a contribution to the development of a significant chemical industry. They were destined for Charles Tennant & Company of St. Rollox in Glasgow. Tennant first came to prominence in 1799 when he patented a process for the manufacture of a bleaching powder, which he sold worldwide. By the 1820s, he had widened the company's chemical activities to include metallurgy and explosives, and, in the 1830s, opened a factory in Fife for the manufacture of sulphuric acid and artificial manures. At the time of the accident, Tennant's St. Rollox factory, extending over one hundred acres, had been described as 'the most important chemical works in the world'.

Contributions to agriculture and horticulture featured in the *Pegasus'* cargo. An unidentified James Sprot was the consignee of ten live sheep, possibly intended as part of a stock breeding programme of a type popular at that time. Casks and bags of seed formed a significant part of the cargo, and the only consignments for which some damage is recorded. Thirty-nine bags of seed were for W. & R. Moubray, Merchants, Leith; three casks of clover seed for R. M. Smith, Merchant, Bernard Street; and George Berry & Co., Importers, were the intended recipients of forty-eight bags and 31 cs of seed. It is possible that so much seed was for onward transmission overseas to Australasia or Canada.

The destination of other seed is clearer – Thomas Cleghorn & Co., who received two bags of seed, ran a noted nursery on the edge of Princes Street Gardens, situated where the Scott Monument now stands. Interestingly, very shortly after the grounding of the *Pegasus*, Cleghorn, who already seems to have been in some financial difficulty, gave up his nursery and emigrated to New Zealand, where he became the Superintendent of the Government Domain at Auckland. Here he laid out grounds for the Governor and the new city, and established both parks and nurseries, supplying the arriving settlers. Was the loss of his seed on the *Pegasus*, possibly the final straw? Certainly, Edinburgh's loss seems to have been New Zealand's gain. Another Edinburgh nursery was due to receive twenty bags of tares. This was Dickson & Co., whose nursery lay on the west side of Inverleith Row. For its day, it was a large commercial nursery:

> An extensive nursery for the rearing and Cultivation of plants, flowers, Shrubs &c ... It is tastefully laid out with flower plots, arbours and ornamental walks, and ranks among the finest nurseries in Scotland.
>
> Ordnance Survey Name Books Ref: OS1/11/85/7

Food and drink were sent by the *Pegasus,* as was soap, which seems to have been retailed exclusively by grocers and wine merchants. Butter was in great demand – twenty-five kegs were for W. & T. Bowe, Leith, Dealers and Grocers, who were also consigned a cask (contents unknown). Other intended recipients of butter were White & Clarke of Leith (ten kegs), James Frier (ten kegs), and William Ford of Kirkgate (ten kegs). Five hogsheads of sugar were destined for two confectioners John Ralph and A. Ferguson, the latter described as 'purveyor of confectionery to her Majesty'. A cask, presumably of wine, was destined for John Gillon & Company, Leith. They had been wine merchants to King William IV, and were also noted for their pioneering development of tinned goods for explorers, equipping the 1838–1843 Antarctic Expedition. Sixteen chests of soap were intended variously for Jamieson & Son, Wine Merchants, in the Grassmarket (twelve); George Sanderson & Co. (three); and James Hill, Grocer and Wine Merchant in the High Street (one).

Other items described only in general terms went to a leather merchant, a shoemaker, a bazaar owner, a stationer, an engraver, two jewellers, a perfumier and two auctioneers.

The cargo as a whole bears witness to Edinburgh's flourishing wholesale and retail trade, but also to industrial and agricultural improvements across Scotland's central belt.

CHAPTER 6

1840–FROM CEMENT TO
BIG CATS AND HORSES

As the new year began, the *Pegasus* was one of a number of vessels involved in assisting shipwrecked sailors. On 27 January 1840, when winds veered west north west, a considerable number of cargo ships left Lowestoft, where they had been held by unfavourable weather, to resume voyages to London. Among them were the brig, the *Quebec* from North Shields, and the schooner, *Regent* from Aberdeen, the latter carrying a cargo of cattle and stone. Just south of Lowestoft, as the ships manoeuvred to get the wind, they collided. The heavily laden *Regent* sank almost immediately. The cargo was lost, but the crew succeeded in leaping on to the *Quebec*. This was perhaps the final straw for the damaged brig, as she also sank, but not before both crews took to her ship's boats. From there the seventeen men were rescued by another Aberdeen ship, the *Bon Accord,* and were disembarked at Great Yarmouth in the middle of the afternoon. There they were assisted by the local branch of the recently formed Shipwrecked Mariners' Society (SMS), who arranged for the men to begin their journey to their home ports aboard the *Albatross,* a paddle steamer belonging to the Norfolk Steam Packet Company and providing a weekly service linking Great Yarmouth, Goole and Hull.

The shipwrecked men disembarked when they reached Hull, where again they were helped by the SMS. Here, the agent was George Moon, a cooper by trade, but a man with a finger in many merchant shipping pies: as well as being an agent for the SMS, he was an insurance agent for Lloyd's, a commissioner for the Humber Pilots, and used by H.M. Revenue & Customs to check the contents of imported barrels of tobacco. He ensured that the Shields and Aberdeen men were provided with money to buy food, and obtained passages for them on the *Pegasus*. She delivered the *Quebec's* crew to North Shields and arrived in Leith with the *Regent's* crew on 31 January 1840.

The *Pegasus* remained in service throughout February, but was withdrawn for a major overhaul at the end of the month. During March, her place was taken on the Leith/Hull route by the P.S. *Foyle*, leased from the Glasgow and Londonderry Steam Packet Company. Taking the ship out of service early in the year was a regular part of her maintenance and does not seem to have had any direct connection with the previous year's grounding. A key feature of the overhaul was the replacement of the ship's two boilers. The need to regularly replace the boilers was a feature of early steamships, and a direct result of how their steam engines worked. The water used to create steam was sea water, and the steam was condensed by spraying more cold sea water into the condensation chamber. Salt water had a corrosive effect on the engine's metalwork, and even worse, salt deposits, which crystallised out during the production of the steam, formed a crust both inside the boiler and in the linking pipework, and reduced the efficiency of the machine. Lastly, as salt deposits increased, so did the salinity of the water, requiring higher temperatures to create the steam. Higher temperatures required more fuel, making the operation of the steamers less economic; but more seriously, they stressed the welding of the boilers, creating the risk of explosion.

The *Pegasus* returned to her station at Leith on 21 May 1840. The next few months seem to have been relatively uneventful. It was a matter of note to the captain, however, that at the end of July, while sailing north, off Whitby, he sailed through a shoal of herring, at least six miles long.

The year saw changes in the business climate. When the *Pegasus* had entered into service at the beginning of 1836, it was generally accepted that the best means of transporting passengers along the east coast was by sea. The distinction of the *Pegasus* was that, as a steam ship, she could perform this task more efficiently than a sailing ship, which was always reliant on favourable winds. In the previous four years, the development of rail travel had altered the situation. The opening of the London – Birmingham line in 1838, brought goods to the Midlands which then could travel on by canal to Hull, increasing the demand on the Company to carry cargo north.

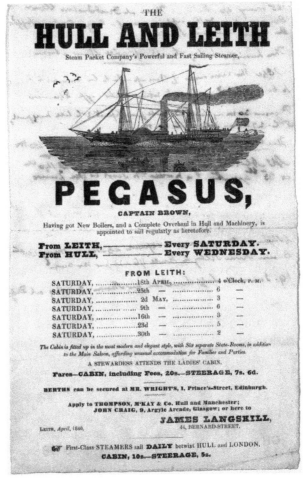

Pegasus Flier 1840
000-100-102-864-C – ©National Museums Scotland

More significantly, in 1840, a direct rail link was opened between London and Hull. Now, both for passengers and freight, Hull was the key interchange on the fastest route north and south; by rail to and from London to Hull, and by ship from Hull to Leith and points north. Although it was to prove to be a short window of opportunity, for the next decade the Company could rely on growing demand to carry both travellers and goods.

The actual building of the railways also contributed to the *Pegasus'* cargo. A letter from the Hull shipping agents, Thompson, McKay & Co. sent to James Langskill of the HLSPC on 18 August 1840, refers to the carriage of ten barrels of cement for Messrs Gibb & Son, Ratho. James Gibb was the Aberdeen engineer whose company was engaged in building the one and a half mile long Almond Valley Viaduct (the longest viaduct in Scotland), which was to carry the high-speed rail trunk line between Edinburgh and Glasgow. The Viaduct did not open until 1842, and, while this is the only surviving record of building materials for it being sent north, it seems likely that items for this major construction were a regular feature of the *Pegasus'* cargo over the next 18 months.

Early September saw two young law clerks, William Fraser and Archy Grant setting off for a holiday jaunt to London. They left Leith on the sixth, and William recorded that his fare to Hull was seven shillings and sixpence, and that he paid a further four pence for both ginger beer and later 'refreshments'. Their attention was particularly attracted by another passenger, travelling with a slave.

Trade may have grown and continued as usual, but for the men and women of the crew, every so often, personal matters took precedence. So it was that on 14 September 1840, the steward on the *Pegasus*, John Smith, was married to Miss Louisa Wilkinson of Hull, at the Roman Catholic Church in the town. Records do not show whether John Smith was the steward on the *Pegasus'* voyage south, leaving Leith on 12 September, but given the lack of employment rights in those days, it is highly probable that he was. The newlyweds probably managed a two-night honeymoon in Hull, before John resumed his duties on the return voyage on the 16 September.

October 1840 saw the *Pegasus* carrying one of her more unusual cargoes – Mr Van Amburgh's Menagerie. Isaac Van Amburgh was an American entrepreneur, who as a young man working with the Zoological Institute of New York, developed considerable skills in training wild animals and in particular lions, tigers and other big cats. In 1834, he formed his own touring menagerie, travelling across the United States. Among his acts, he rode on the back of a lion and stuck his head into its mouth (though not both at the same time!). In 1838, he brought his show to Britain, and when Queen Victoria visited it eleven times in 1839, its popularity was assured.

In the autumn of 1840, Van Amburgh embarked on a British tour with his Menagerie. Generally, the performances with his animals were part of a broader programme of entertainment, the animal tableaux being interspersed with plays, ballets and opera and/or individual singers and dancers. Travelling on from successful performances in Birmingham, Van Amburgh opened in Hull for two performances at the *Theatre Royal* on 19 October 1840. From there the show was transferring to Edinburgh.

On 21 October, the Menagerie was loaded on to the *Pegasus* for the voyage to Edinburgh, where the show was due to open at Edinburgh's *Theatre Royal* on Tuesday 27 October. Sadly, there are no descriptions of how this was achieved, but both the departure from Hull and the arrival at Leith must have provided a fascinating spectacle for onlookers. Apart from the Van Amburgh company – the man himself, his assistants and the animal keepers, two large performance cages and at least three lions, two leopards and a tigress, around whom Van Amburgh's tableaux centred, must have been loaded, possibly more. How did they travel? It was customary when sending wild animals on long journeys to build them individual crates, but was this done for what was only a twenty-four-hour journey? It seems possible that they were simply loaded on to the ship in their individual metal barred cages, in which they would have travelled if the journey had been by land. How were the cages put aboard? Did they stay on deck or were they lowered into the hold, and if so, how? What did the other passengers make of their travelling companions? Fortunately, the voyage was without incident, and the animals disembarked safely at Leith on the Friday. Given Van Amburgh's track record as a showman, it is probable that they then processed up the hill to Edinburgh and were quartered somewhere near the *Theatre Royal*.

Wisely, the first show at the *Theatre Royal* did not open until the following Tuesday, allowing the animals to recover from their unusual travelling conditions on the voyage, but when it did, the audience were not disappointed. On 28 October, *The Scotsman* reported:

> The exhibition is one of a novel and certainly very striking character. After a short introductory scene, from which we learn that a certain 'Roman Captive' (Mr Van Amburgh) has been condemned to be devoured by wild beasts, the curtain drew up and exhibited a beautiful collection of lions, leopards, and tigers, in two large cages, occupying the whole breadth of the stage. The great lion-tamer soon entered, and went through a variety of manoeuvres with the animals – now resting or standing on them – now lying down and embracing them – at one moment causing them to mount on his shoulders, and occasionally irritating and making them growl fearfully. With the lions he makes particularly free, tearing open their jaws and placing his neck or arm in their mouths, and all the while preserving considerable grace in his motions, and forming at times very interesting tableaux. The animals themselves are well worth seeing, and the tameness they exhibit is truly wonderful. Mr Van Amburgh was loudly applauded at the close of his performance.

Van Amburgh and the Lions. Engraving after Landseer's painting.

In addition to the 'Roman Captive', a second tableau, 'Mungo Park', had been added to the repertoire, but due to difficulties with the stage machinery, there was a delay in performing this at the theatre. The company, however provided other entertainment for the citizens of Edinburgh. They could attend animal feeding sessions in the afternoons before the evening performances. According to one witness, in *The Scotsman* of 31 October 1840, the feeding 'exhibits them, as it were, in the act of seizing their prey; and the ferocity they manifest shows that their natural spirit is not wholly subdued'.

Meanwhile, in November 1840, the *Pegasus* was involved in a near accident with the *Vesta,* a steamer belonging to the Newcastle Steam Navigation Company, which in 1840 was sailing the Leith/ Newcastle route. The incident took place off North Sunderland, on 14 November, in heavy seas, as both ships were sailing south. They had successfully navigated the Inner Passage through the Farne Islands and were sailing abreast as they passed Sunderland Point, with the *Vesta* seaward of the *Pegasus*. According to a passenger on the *Pegasus*, the *Pegasus* was close to shore, when the *Vesta* overtook her, cutting across her bow only ten yards ahead, ignoring Captain Brown's signals and causing great distress to the passengers. The incident was viewed very differently by a passenger on the *Vesta*. According to him, neither ship was close to shore – three miles out and abreast, and the cause of the accident was the *Pegasus* adjusting her sails in an attempt to gain an advantage. As a result, she crossed into the path of the *Vesta*. As there was no accident, there was no enquiry so where the blame actually lay must remain unclear. The *Vesta* passenger's irate letter, however, contained a telling phrase – 'It would be well to avoid rivalry, particularly with inferior vessels of this description, as it is evident that this feeling was the cause of placing the Pegasus in the situation ...'[3]

As was claimed in 1836, was the near accident the result of two ships racing to gain advantage? Also was the *Pegasus* an inferior ship? The *Vesta*, built at Newcastle, had gone into service just a year after the *Pegasus*, and initially had sailed from Newcastle to both Leith and Hull, so could certainly be considered a rival. She was overall a bigger ship, equipped with two 75 horsepower engines, compared with the *Pegasus*' single engine. Ten feet longer and six feet broader, she was capable of carrying 300 tons, as opposed to the *Pegasus*' 130. Although bare statistics do not tell the whole story, it seems likely that the *Pegasus* was now outclassed.

In December, the *Pegasus* was again involved in bringing entertainment to Edinburgh, this time as part of the Christmas and New Year festivities. On this occasion she carried Mr Ducrow's Equestrian Theatre. Andrew Ducrow had been born in London into a performance family in 1793 – his father, a strongman, was known as the 'Flemish Hercules'. Andrew, however, excelled in

---

3 From letters published in the *Shipping and Mercantile Gazette* 21 and 28 November 1840.

horse riding, and following the early death of his father in about 1808, he, together with his brothers and sisters, travelled abroad, learning their trade in circuses in Belgium and France, before Andrew formed his own circus company. He returned to London in 1823, and after performing at *Sadlers Wells*, he bought *Astley's Amphitheatre* in London, which became the base for his company for the next two decades. Ducrow himself became known as the 'Colossus of Equestrianism' and was noted for his daring riding performances and his willingness to perform any of the acts expected of his performers. He enjoyed the patronage of both King William IV (who created a private performance area for him at the Brighton Pavilion) and Queen Victoria. By 1840, Ducrow had acquired a second arena in Edinburgh – the *Royal Amphitheatre of Arts* in Nicolson Street, where Edinburgh's *Festival Theatre* now stands, and performed seasonally there. By now, he was joined in his performances by his wife, a noted equestrian in her own right, and his young son.

Ducrow's Equestrian Theatre travelled to Hull from touring engagements at Leicester and Derby, to board the *Pegasus* on 16 December. This time there was a full party of performers, together with props and costumes. One of the acts was to be a re-creation of the Knights' Tournament from Walter Scott's *Ivanhoe*, so there must have been a considerable amount of equipment and scenery to be stowed aboard, as well as the horses and ponies. The exact number of horses is never specified, but as the ship was accustomed to carrying horses for the army, this should have been less challenging than Van Amburgh's cats. Again, the boarding of the ship must have provided quite a spectacle for the onlookers, and at least one horse proved to have a mind of its own, as reported in *The Hull Packet* of 18 December 1840 – it 'could not be induced to quit the pier … On the man who was in charge of them coming up, and speaking one word in a tone of command, – the proud animal yielded, and walked on board, submissive as a child'.

The voyage was completed successfully, and the company and their equipment disembarked. They opened to great acclaim at his *Amphitheatre* on 21 December:

> This place of amusement opened on Monday with a fine display of horsemanship and other exercises of the arena. The house has been tastefully decorated, and arranged with due regard to the comfort of the audience. Among the performances, we may mention the evolutions of Le Petit Ducrow on horseback, as free, rapid, and graceful. Great admiration was also excited by the exhibition of Madame Ducrow's finely-trained pony, 'Beauty'.
>
> *The Scotsman* 23 December 1840

> The whole concluded with a representation of the Tournament of Ashby-de-la-Zouch, as described in Ivanhoe, aided by stage effect and appropriate scenery. The spectacle, which has been produced at a great expense, was remarkable for the splendour of the costumes, and the glitter of the trappings and decorations. The combat was also sustained with great spirit, to which the high training of the horses, of course, greatly contributed.
>
> *Caledonian Mercury* 24 December1840

Overall, it had been a busy and successful year for the *Pegasus*. It would be good to think that at least some of the crew, between sailings, were able to enjoy the entertainments they had brought to Edinburgh. As Ducrow was incapacitated by a severe stroke the following year, any of those who got to the *Royal Amphitheatre* would have been privileged to see one of the last performances of the 'Father of British Circus Equestrianism'.

CHAPTER 7

1841 – A TIME OF CHANGE

1841 was to mark a significant change in the development of the HLSPC, and with it, the fortunes of the *Pegasus*. This change, however, had its origins in developments at Hull the previous year. At the beginning of July 1840, the Selby/Hull railway line was opened. Hull's wish to be connected to central England had been a long time in coming to fruition. A line to Leeds had been surveyed as early as 1824 but had not attracted sufficient shareholders to be carried forward. In 1834, a line opened between Leeds and Selby, but goods or passengers for onward transit then had to be taken by steamer to Hull, to connect with the east coast shipping routes. The arrival of the railway at Selby, however, gave a new impetus to the plan for a rail link to Hull and a further survey was carried out in 1834, before application was made to parliament for an Act to authorise the railway. The process was delayed by a series of objections from:

» the Hull Corporation who believed they controlled the development rights of the foreshore
» Robert Raikes[4], a Hull banker, and, by marriage, squire of Welton, through which the intended line would pass, who

---

4 Raikes, who, as a younger man, had been responsible for the development of the Sunday School movement, concluded his petition thus 'AN APPEAL is therefore made to Parliament to protect private property from the unrelenting encroachment of speculation, and a Land Owner from being compelled by the Legislature, contrary to the General Principles of Law, to sell his Property, for the purpose of Establishing a Nuisance to himself from which Others are to derive the gain'.

claimed that the railway would lower the value of his property at Welton, and spoil his view of the Humber

» a group of Sabbatarians who wished the use of the line banned on Sundays.

Despite these objections, in 1836 parliament passed an Act authorising a line from Selby to Hull, and it opened in a downpour of rain on 1 July 1840. From the beginning, the driving force had been to provide a link between the industrial towns of Lancashire and Yorkshire, through Hull, to the markets served by the east coast steamers. With this in mind, the new railway station, known as Manor House Street Station, was built, not in the centre of the town, but on the quayside, for ease of transfer to the various shipping lines.

Manor House Street Station. Hull Packet 3 July 1840

This then was the background to the Company's notice which appeared in both Scottish and Yorkshire newspapers at the end of January 1841:

> The powerful First Class Steamer, GLENALBYN, having been purchased for the increased Accommodation of the Trade, is ready to be placed on the Station, and early in Spring will Sail alternately with the PEGASUS, leaving each end Twice every Week, namely, every Wednesday and Saturday.

At a stroke, the company had doubled its sailing capacity.

The *Glenalbyn,* which now joined the *Pegasus* on the Leith/Hull route, had been built in 1834. She was a two masted wooden paddle steamer with two engines providing 110 horsepower. At 121 feet four inches in length, she was a slightly shorter ship but was both a foot broader and one and a half feet deeper than the *Pegasus.* She had been built for the Glenalbyn Steam Boat Company, based in Tobermory, Isle of Mull, to sail along the west coast, providing a service between Liverpool and Inverness, by way of Islay, Oban, Fort William and the Caledonian Canal. Then, much as Caledonia MacBrayne, the current operators of the west coast ferries do today, the company combined the carriage of goods and passengers with the tourism trade. In 1834, the *Glenalbyn* became the first steamship to visit St. Kilda on a tour which also took in ruined coastal castles, a spar cave on Skye, Fingal's Cave on Staffa, and Iona[5]. Perhaps business needs and tourism did not mix well, for, in 1838, she was sold to the General Shipping Company, Berwick-upon-Tweed, to sail from Berwick to both Leith and Hull. Reportedly the Berwick Company found her too expensive to operate, and throughout 1840, she was chartered to a Hull company, Wilson, Hudson & Co., to provide mail services from Hull to Norway and Sweden. An account of a sailing to Norway in November 1840, described the ship as 'small ... but there was no appearance of leakiness or discomfort'; but once out of port 'the vessel rolled much during the night' and on the two days following[6], before passengers thankfully arrived at Christiansand.

It was certainly in the Company's interest to increase their fleet on the Hull/Leith route, but exactly why they chose to acquire the *Glenalbyn* is not clear. Not only was she older than the *Pegasus* but her years sailing up heavy seas of the west coast would have

<hr />

5 *Caledonian Mercury* 25 August 1834.
6 *Liverpool Mail,* 17 November 1840.

taken their toll, and, as we have seen, she did not sail well in bad weather. She would have been known to the Company's shipping agents, Thompson McKay, through her work for the Berwick company, and presumably they thought her a suitable vessel. When, in February 1841, Lloyd's surveyed her at Hull, as she was loading for her return voyage to Leith, the surveyor noted on the form – 'This vessel appears to be constructed of Materials for 7 years A1 by the Tables, but the time not admitting of a very close examination' – not entirely a ringing endorsement. It may have been that a deciding factor in acquiring the *Glenalbyn*, was that they were removing a possible competitor from their route. Given the ship's history over the previous three years – sold to the *General Shipping Company* which found she did not suit, and chartered for the Scandinavian mail route, where presumably she also was found not to suit, she was probably a reasonably cheap purchase.

A new ship also meant a new master. For reasons which are never explained in the records, it was decided that John Brown, who had commanded the *Pegasus* since autumn 1839, now took charge of the *Glenalbyn*. The man who took over the *Pegasus* was Alexander Miller. Definite information about Miller is limited, but from 1835 to 1839 he had been the master of the Leith smack *Trusty*, carrying passengers and goods between Leith and London, on a series of generally uneventful voyages. In 1838, south of Spurn Point, he recovered a large figurehead floating in the water; in 1839, the *Trusty* lost an anchor while sheltering from a gale at Harwich, but Miller retrieved it on the return voyage. In 1839, the smack's owners decided to have her remodelled as a schooner, and presumably Miller was out of a job while this work was carried out. Some accounts state that he first joined the *Pegasus* as mate in 1839/40. He was clearly a competent master of a sailing vessel and could be seen as a 'safe pair of hands'. He must have known well the east coast route between Leith and London, but had he any experience of steamships before taking over the *Pegasus*?

It was not just the Company's sailing arrangements, but also its actual structure that changed at this time. On 1 February 1841, Robert Barclay retired from the Company, although continuing to operate his own shipbuilding business. As a result, the Company was reformed with six partners, although retaining the name of the Hull and Leith Steam Packet Company. The main features of the new agreement were:

» Thomas Barclay was the majority shareholder with 49/64^{ths} of the shares.
» The remainder were divided amongst Robert Cook, his brother-in-law (4/64^{ths}); John Brown, captain of the *Pegasus* (2/64^{ths}); James Langskill, the Company's shipping agent in Leith (2/64^{ths}), and John MacKay (4/64^{ths}) and Henry Stead (3/64^{ths}), both described as Manchester wharfingers, but actually the representatives of Thompson McKay & Co., the shipping agents at the Hull end.
» James Langskill would be employed as the Company's shipping agent at Leith on a salary of £100 per annum.
» There would be quarterly Board Meetings.
» On the expiry of the insurance, the two ships would be reinsured at a sum of at least two thirds of their estimated value.

The capital of the Company at this point was stated to be £5,500, which included the current insurance, due to expire in August, landing box stages, sailing boards, office furniture and all other effects of the *Pegasus* and the Leith office, together with the *Glenalbyn*, valued at her purchase price (unfortunately not specified).

The re-formed Company now needed to ensure that their investment in the second ship brought in the anticipated profits. As the spring progressed, a customised advertising campaign was launched. In Scotland, the advantages of the new rail link at Hull, and the ease of access to a range of different markets were highlighted to potential customers. On 29 April 1841, the *Fife Herald* advertised the route under the heading:

TWICE A WEEK TO HULL, YORK, MANCHESTER, LEEDS, SHEFFIELD, LONDON, and the EASTERN and MIDLAND COUNTIES of ENGLAND.

After giving details of the sailing times and fares further details were provided:

From Hull there are both Railway and Canal Conveyances to Bradford, Birmingham, Derby, Halifax, Huddersfield, Leeds, Liverpool, Leicester, Manchester, Nottingham, the Potteries, Rochdale, Sheffield, Wakefield, York, &c. &c. The Canal Rates much reduced by the Railway competition; to London, Railway daily; and Steam Five Days a-week, Cabin, 10s.6d.; Steerage, 5s.

In England, the focus was on the potential to visit the highland lochs and scenery, beloved of Queen Victoria, and described by Walter Scott. Special return rates were offered for what we would now describe as 'short breaks'. Typical was that carried by the *Leeds Mercury* on Saturday 22 May 1841, headed:

TREAT DURING WHITSUN WEEK.
TO LEITH AND BACK FOR ONE FARE.

...

Passengers leaving Hull on the 29th May, and 2nd June, and returning from Leith on the 5th and 9th June, will only be charged *one Fare* for the PASSAGE TO LEITH AND BACK.

From Leith or Edinburgh there are Daily direct Conveyances by Land and Water, to the Lochs, Mountains, and all Parts of Scotland.

The first quarterly meeting of the board took place on 10 May 1841, and was largely taken up with the condition of the *Glenalbyn*, including damage to her boilers. The cost of refit and repairs to her was estimated at some £400. With £720 in the banks, this was not a problem, but nevertheless it was decided for the present to pay no dividends. It may also have given the shareholders second thoughts about their recent purchase.

Matters seem to have improved by the next board meeting on 13 August. Accounts now showed a balance of £2,500, with outstanding expenses of only £400-500. Arrangements were also made for reinsuring the *Pegasus* with The Forth Marine Insurance Company and the Glasgow Marine Insurance Company – valuing the ship at £4,500. The main agenda item however was the acquisition of a new ship. Thomas Barclay produced a model of the proposed boat, and stated that he expected to receive estimates for its costs the following week. He said that Captain Cook agreed with him that it was now 'a favourable opportunity for ordering a new Iron Boat from cheapness of Iron & present slackness among Engineers in Glasgow'. So, the matter was decided, and a decision was taken to have the new boat ready for service by July 1842. Despite this proposed extra expenditure, it was agreed to pay a £5 dividend per share for the preceding half year.

Another feature of the changed business organisation was that the running costs of the *Pegasus* were formally recorded. Although by no means complete, they give some insights into the amount of coal necessary to fuel the steamer and its related cost. It would of course always be a variable, since in favourable weather she would rely at least in part on her sails.

DATE	TYPE OF COAL	TONNAGE	COST
13 July 1841	Engine Hard Coals	11.5	£6.6s.6d
28 July 1841	Engine Hard Coals	14	£7.14s.0d
11 August 1841	Engine Hard Coals	15.5	£8.10s.6d
16 August 1841	Steam Coal	18	£9.4s.6d
24 August 1841	Engine Hard Coals	19.25	£10.11s.9d
5 October 1841	Engine Hard Coals	18.5	£10.14s.6d
19 October 1841	Engine Hard Coals	22.5	£12.7s.6d
3 November 1841	Engine Hard Coals	18	£9.18s.0d
16 November 1841	Engine Hard Coals	21.75	£11.19s.3d
24 November 1841	Engine Hard Coals	14	£7.14s.0d

It would seem that generally a load of coal lasted for two return voyages and, at its dearest, it cost just over £12. Assuming an average passenger load of fifty, even if all passengers travelled steerage, the minimum passenger income for these four trips would be £75; to which should be added income from the carriage of goods. Even allowing for the additional costs of crew etc. for which there are no records, at this time the HLSPC must certainly have been a very profitable business.

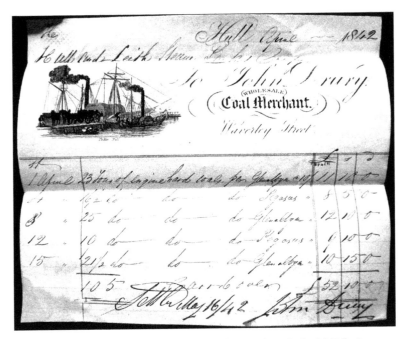

Bill of Coals 1842 – University of Glasgow Library, Archives & Special Collections,

CHAPTER 8

ABOARD THE PEGASUS 1841

As usual, at the start of a new year the *Pegasus* was due for an overhaul. This year, however, it was delayed until the *Glenalbyn* came into service in February 1841, the Company calculating that if this were done, it would avoid the need for hiring a replacement. So it was, that about nine p.m. on the evening of Monday 25 January, when the *Pegasus* was moored at the quay in Hull, someone described as 'a countryman' fell into the water from the pier. His cries for help were heard by the ship's engineer, who grabbed a lifebuoy from outside the *Minerva Tavern*, and threw it to the drowning man. With its help, the man was able to keep himself afloat until a rescue boat could reach him.

All the participants remain anonymous, and yet this rescue, of a type common wherever there is water the careless might fall into, was in fact quite historic. Alexander Gordon Carte, an ordnance storekeeper at the Citadel military fort in Hull, invented the life buoy during the 1830s, but it was not used before 1838, and this account of the rescue in 1841 is the first recorded account of its successful deployment. The rescued man was certainly lucky, as the Dock company had only installed the lifebuoy outside the inn in September 1840, for without it, on a cold, dark, January night, there might have been a very different outcome to the accident.

The *Pegasus* refit seems to have been completed during February and March 1841, with no issues identified. She returned to service, and to her new captain, Alexander Miller, some time in April.

Within the month, there had been an accident. In preparing to leave Leith harbour, the ship had struck the Martello Tower, known locally as the 'Tally Toor'. The tower, one of a series round the British coast, had been built in 1809, during the Napoleonic Wars, to protect the entrance to the harbour, at a time when the fear of a French invasion seemed a real possibility.

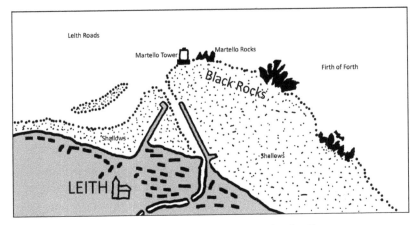

Sketch of Leith harbour based on 1842 Admiralty Chart

While protecting the entrance, as can be seen from the map, it also reduced room for manoeuvre on leaving the narrow entrance of the harbour, particularly for ships travelling south. Once clear of the pier, they had to make a tight right turn, to avoid both the Tower and the dangerous Black Rocks. Miller was an experienced captain and the Tower stood 13.8 metres high, not the sort of obstacle one was likely to miss, but the *Pegasus* was a significantly larger ship than the smack he had previously captained. Records make no mention of adverse conditions, but either thick fog or a strong onshore wind could have contributed to the error. It was not a good beginning, and resulted in the crews being instructed to '*maintain the utmost vigilance*'. Fortunately, the damage done to the ship was much less than originally anticipated – only some thirty or forty shillings, according to the Company minutes.

The middle of May brought excitement of an altogether more enjoyable type for the ship and her crew, when the Royal Mail Ship *Forth* was launched at Leith. In 1840, the Admiralty had begun a programme of shipbuilding and subsidy for ships to carry the Royal Mail across the globe. The intent was that these ships, as well as carrying the mail, could serve as war ships in times of trouble. No expense was spared to ensure that the ships built were of a standard fit for both roles. They were described as:

> tall handsome wooden ships, sitting very lofty on the water, and rigged proportionately to their bulk ... engined by the best makers; they were richly furnished within, and without they looked as imposing as men-o-war[7].

Like the *Pegasus,* these were paddle ships which carried sail, but there the similarity ended. The *Forth* was 1,900 tons gross (1,147 tons register), with 450 horsepower, 245 feet long and 30 feet deep. Robert Menzies and Sons, shipbuilders of Leith, had successfully won the contract to build the *Forth* for the West India Royal Mail Steam Company. It was by far the largest ship ever to have been built at Leith. On Saturday 19 May 1841, she was due to be launched.

Not surprisingly, there was tremendous interest in the launch. From early morning, people from across all of Edinburgh and beyond, crowded into Leith for the event – at the time it was calculated that some 60,000 people were present. Anticipating that such a crush would create difficulties for the 'great and the good' among the spectators, arrangements had been made for them to have places on three of the service steamers moored in the harbour, the *Pegasus,* the *Royal William* (transatlantic Liverpool/New York) and the *Royal Victoria* (a Clyde steamer). Otherwise, people made out as best they could. *The Scotsman* described the bustling scene:

---

7 W. Clarke Russell, *The Ship – Her Story*

The extensive line of pier, the various craft, great and small, stationed or cruising about in the harbour, many of which were decorated with flags, the sea-wall of the docks, the house-tops, wherever a peep of the new ship could be obtained, all were crowded with spectators. For ourselves we were among the favoured few – there were perhaps a thousand of us – admitted into the yard of Messrs Menzies, the enterprising builders (*where a viewing platform had been built*); and there was the ponderous fabric before us, propped up on dry land, adorned with innumerable flags, and seemingly 'straining upon the slip.' All was bustle and preparation – wondering which was the best place, and bobbing about to try various points, until almost every point was occupied; in the midst of which, faint huzzas came from seemingly impatient groups at a distance, and the band of the 29th flattered the air with soft music.

26 May 1841

In the struggle to obtain a good viewpoint, the *Pegasus* became the centre of a minor fracas, when, as her crew sought to adjust her mooring rope at the quayside, spectators already on the quay objected that the ship's movement would block their view. All, however, seems to have been resolved peacefully.

About two p.m. the shipyard workers began the process of removing the props holding the *Forth* in place. As three o'clock approached, Mr Menzies brought a young lady, Miss Colville, the daughter of the Deputy Chairman of the West India Royal Mail Steam Company, to the bow of the ship. There he handed her a small ribbon decorated bottle, attached by a cord to the ship. Taking it in her hand, she threw it against the ship's figurehead, and named the ship the *Forth*. Duly named, the ship slid gracefully into the water, to the accompaniment of cannon fire, and, for good luck, the ships' carpenters threw their hammers in after her. It was a matter of surprise to the reporters who watched the scene, that despite the huge crowds, there were no accidents, and the crowds dispersed peacefully, some returning home, others continuing to the nearby

S4622: The launch of the Steam Packet 'Forth', 22 May 1841 (detail).
©National Maritime Museum, Greenwich, London

village of Newhaven to enjoy the long-established seaside treat of a fish supper. For the *Pegasus* and her crew, all that remained was to get the ship moved to her normal mooring, and cleaned and tidied for her sailing the following Wednesday.

Summer sailings were uneventful, and sadly there is no record of how successful the tourist promotions launched at the beginning of the season were. In September 1841, both the *Pegasus* and the *Glenalbyn* carried to Hull parts of a consignment of Cheviot Wool, ordered by Samuel Eastwood and Son, Woolstaplers, Huddersfield, from Messrs Adam and Russell, Wool Dealers and Skinners, of Bonnington, Edinburgh, for onward delivery to Huddersfield. At the time, it was simply another routine piece of cargo. Unfortunately, between the time of the purchase of the wool and its delivery, Samuel Eastwood became bankrupt, and the wool was to become the subject of a significant Leeds Court Case the following year, with publicity for the ships.

In October 1841, the crew of the *Pegasus* could look forward to enjoying the excitement and entertainment of the Hull Fair. Originally founded by a charter from King Edward I in the thirteenth century, this annual fair ran from the Friday nearest 11 October until a week on the Saturday, with many of the highlights taking place on the Monday and Tuesday. This was a large-scale event, with attractions and markets across the town, and visitors coming from far afield.

A contemporary account describes three streets filled with market stalls selling everything from sweets and fruits to clothes, toys and patent medicines. Side shows were set up on the Dock Green and included swing boats, dancing monkeys, and a giant. Along Railway Street, there were two large, illuminated song and dance booths, where the public could dance to named vocalists. In competition with them were two travelling theatres, a menagerie, a circus, and Thiodon's *Theatre of Arts* presenting moving panoramas of important events and foreign cities. Illuminations at the

Zoological Gardens, enhanced by a firework display, the centre-piece of which was *St. George & the Dragon*, provided yet more attractions. All local businesses – shops, eating houses and pubs took full advantage of the influx of visitors. That year the *Pegasus* docked at Hull on Sunday 10 October. Conveniently, sabbatarianism ensured the Fair was closed on the Sabbath, so disembarking was not a problem. Once the ship was cleaned and prepared for its return voyage on the Wednesday, the crew could join the locals and other visitors in exploring 'all the fun of the fair'.

On this occasion, however, the fair was not fun for all. As was, and is often the case at such events, there were those who celebrated not wisely but too well. One of these was Thomas Reading, a 65 year-old Hull fish seller, who, at about seven p.m. on the Monday evening, left the fair none too steadily. A small boy, Charles Foreman, on his way to the fair, saw Reading stumble as he reached the lock

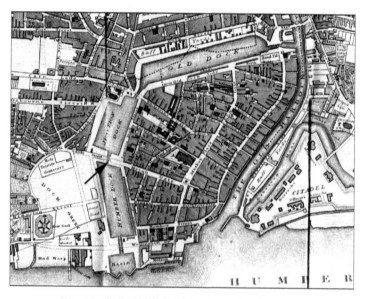

River Humber and Hull Docks showing the lock (arrowed) at Mytongate Bridge – From Greenwood's Picture of Hull 1835

at Mytongate Bridge, catch the edge of the lock with his thighs and fall headlong into the water in the lock pit. A lifebuoy, which had been placed by the lock for such emergencies, was missing from its hook.

When the alarm was raised, the first to arrive on the scene was the duty policeman, Richard Stamp, who came armed with a boat hook, but only managed to hook Reading's hat – there was no sign of the body. Next came William Hudson, the Docks' foreman for the Mytongate Bridge, bringing grappling irons with him. He had heard a splash while on duty in the Watch House. It was, however, one of the *Pegasus'* crew who took charge at this point, taking the grappling irons from Mr Hudson, and with the help of Stamp, they raised Reading's body after some fifteen to twenty minutes. Surprisingly, the crewman was not called to give evidence at the inquest, held the following day at the *Junction Tavern*, so who it was remains a mystery. Considering the way Reading fell into the lock, probably there was nothing that could have been done to rescue him alive, but with lifesaving equipment by the lock, and dock watchmen on duty, it seems unsatisfactory that it took twenty minutes and a sailor from the *Pegasus* to rescue the body.

October 1841 proved to be an eventful month for the *Pegasus* in other ways too. A week after the fair, she set sail for Leith on Wednesday, 20 October, at the tail end of what had been a serious storm. All seemed to go well until she reached Whitby, at which point her engine failed, and, relying solely on her sails, she was forced back to take shelter in Bridlington Bay. At this point, several of her passengers disembarked, returning to Hull with lurid accounts of the voyage. The shipping agents, Thompson McKay, sent word of events to James Langskill at Leith:

Hull, 21st October 1841
The Peg. was telegraphed as per enclosed (*no enclosure survives in the records*) by today's post & this Evg. Mr Raith & 2 Gent. returned from her having come off at Burlington (*the old name*

for Bridlington). They bring sad accounts of the weather. The
Engine they say would not work & she has in consequence come
back from off Whitby. Her cabin windows were broken & the
Forecastle all aswim, but we presume a little latitude may be
given to a 'Travellers' report. The weather has been however
tremendous, and I am glad she has got into a place of safety. It is
now moderate & she will be able to proceed. If there is any danger of the Boiler or valves giving way, let her be laid up at once
for the boat will lose more in character than on the money she
will make. It is getting widely known that her boilers are ten-
der. Let us know on her arrival whether her cargo is damaged.

University of Glasgow Library, Archives & Special
Collections UGD255/4/35/1

There are no records of damage to the cargo, but certainly the ship
itself seems to have had significant physical damage, and, equally important, it was another blow to her reputation. She continued sailing until the end of November 1841, but then was withdrawn from service for two months for repair at Hull. Details of
the repairs are vague, but in the minutes of the Company's board
meeting in February 1842, there is a reference to 'the great repair
done the *Pegasus* at Hull', as part of the costs for 1841. The records
also show November bills from John Hall of Barton Ropery for
'Ropes taking out Boilers etc.' together with 15.5 yards of No. 3
Canvas, presumably to replace damaged sails. There is no record
of exactly who carried out the actual engine repair in Hull, nor
its cost; but the work was probably undertaken by Brownlow,
Pearson and Co. of Humber Bank, the settling of whose accounts
took Thomas Barclay on a special trip to Hull to obtain 'the best
possible terms' in the summer of 1842. While the *Pegasus* was out
of service, the opportunity was taken to give her what her owners described as 'a complete overhaul', including 'every modern
improvement'. Again, details of what this meant are lacking, but
one relevant item in the Company archives is for dyeing fringes
crimson, so presumably her cabin furnishings etc. were being up-
graded. She would not go back into service until 9 February 1842.

CHAPTER 9

1842–DEVELOPING THE COMPANY

On 31 January 1842, there was an extraordinary meeting of the Company's board at Leith. Thomas Barclay, Captains Cook and Brown, and James Langskill, the Company manager, were present, and Mr Langskill held a letter authorising a proxy vote on behalf of Thompson, McKay, the Hull shipping agents. The meeting centred on the building of the new ship, which had been agreed in principle back in 1840. Although not recorded in the surviving 1841 minutes, a decision must have been taken to give the business to Thomas Wingate & Company, of Whiteinch on the Clyde, and James Langskill had previously been instructed to make enquiries as to the reputation of Wingate's in Glasgow. There was perhaps some reason for uncertainty. They had begun as iron founders about 1820 but had diversified into shipbuilding at Whiteinch in 1832.

During the next decade, they had developed skills both in the making and fitting of steam engines, and in building iron ships. They had attracted attention by providing engines for the *Sirius*, which, in 1838, became the first paddle steamer to cross the Atlantic to New York, arriving there several hours ahead of Brunel's more famous *Great Western*. In 1840, this success was followed up by the launch of the *Henrietta*, the first iron seagoing sailing vessel built in Scotland. Nevertheless, in terms of shipbuilding, they could be regarded as relative newcomers, and, with their use of new materials, the durability of their ships was still open to question. Thomas Barclay, however, had been very keen that his company should be seen once more at the forefront of developments.

Somewhere in the system, however, arrangements had slipped up – the HLSPC had defaulted on the first instalment due to Wingate's. By the time of the meeting, Barclay had made a payment of £900 on account, and the board now agreed to pay £1,100, the outstanding part of the first instalment, to write an apology for the inconvenience caused to Wingate's, and offer payment of a second instalment, making arrangements, if necessary, to borrow funds from the bank. Mr Langskill reported that, having made enquiries through the bank, 'Messrs Wingate & Co. stood very well in Glasgow!' The rest of the meeting was taken up with considerable debate on the necessity of a formal detailed contract, possibly incurring considerable legal expenses, as urged by Thompson, McKay, or on whether a detailed specification and Letter of Agreement, which would include a clause that the building was to be supervised by the Company's architect, Mr Denny, was sufficient. The decision was left in abeyance until the scheduled February board meeting, but, in the meantime, Mr Langskill was asked to investigate what advantages there could be in having a lawyer draw up the specification.

The scheduled quarterly meeting followed five days later, on Saturday, 5 February. This time only Thomas Barclay and James Langskill were present. Mr Langskill presented an incomplete financial statement, since the bills for the *Pegasus* repairs had not yet been received, but this showed that the net earnings of the *Pegasus* and *Glenalbyn* together amounted to some £4,960 – a minimum of £458,600 in today's money. Although Mr Langskill was confident that there was scope for the Hull and Leith trade to grow still further, he nevertheless felt that, in view of the ever-increasing depreciation of the two existing ships, it would be appropriate to sell one or the other when the new vessel came into service. Following up on the previous meeting, he had made further enquiries regarding Wingate's and had received further good reports both from banks and from Wingate's' shareholders.

Thomas Barclay then reported on the new ship. Work there was being carefully monitored by both himself and the marine architect, William Denny, with Captain Cook, and 'other parties of experience' being used as sounding boards for improvements etc. The meeting ended with the conclusion that the agreement, the plans and models, and the superintendence of Mr Denny were sufficient to secure a good job, and that 'legal interference or an attempt to more precisely specify the work ... might lead to a misunderstanding[8]'.

Plans for the Company's new vessel, and ensuring adequate trade to justify its expense, were to be the main issues as the year progressed. Already, in April, the new ship was advertised:

> The *New Iron Steam-Packet Ship* building for this Trade is now in state of forwardness. *Her Large Dimensions* and *Great Power* will secure increased speed for Passengers, and ample room for cargo, as well heavy as light goods.
>
> *Fife Herald*, 21 April 1842

The board meeting took place on 7 May 1842. Thomas Barclay reported that the new ship was almost completely plated, and the engines and boilers were also 'in a state of forwardness'. The balance in the banks was now £2,300 – the drop from February probably due to the bills now paid for the repairs to the *Pegasus*. Nevertheless, they decided to offer Wingate's the second instalment for the build, as it had not been taken up in January.

On 7 June 1842, James Langskill died at home in Leith. As this was before statutory death registration in Scotland, there is no record of the cause of death, but since he was only thirty, and left no will, it may be assumed that it was unexpected.

---

8 University of Glasgow Library, Archives & Special Collections, Minutes of the Hull & Leith Steam Packet Company UGD 255/4/2/1

Langskill had joined the company in 1839, having previously been the Edinburgh shipping agent for the London/Leith Shipping Company. At the time of his death, he left a widow, Elizabeth, and three children, Elizabeth (9), Robert (8) and Margaret (7). Robert Barclay subsequently became involved under a Scottish procedure known as *Executor Dative qua*, applying to take over possession and management of Langskill's personal and moveable estate (amounting to £444.5s.2d), on the grounds that Langskill had owed him £100. Legal papers do not explain the basis of this debt, and since Langskill's life was insured for £100, and he held shares in the company, valued at £302, it is possible that this legal procedure was not about taking money from the widow and her children, but was rather a means of enabling the estate to be efficiently wound up. This would accord with Robert Barclay's reputation for helping the needy, and the fact that, as soon as Langskill's son, Robert, was old enough, he was found a place as a clerk in the Company's office.

With Langskill's death, records for the next two months are limited, but it was a period of significant developments. Building on the existing promotion of the Leith/Hull route as a means of access to the Midlands and North West, there had been negotiations with the railway companies to develop a system of through fares. These came to fruition by July 1842, when new notices advertised reduced fares from Leith to Manchester, Leeds, Bradford, Huddersfield, Halifax, Rochdale, Wakefield &c. with an all-in price for travel to any place on the Manchester & Leeds Railway.

Fife Herald 14 July 1842

» Cabin and Second Class Train 25s.
» Cabin and Third Class Train 20s.
» Steerage and Third Class Train 13s.

At this time, the Company also recruited an additional captain for the increased fleet. This was Alexander Blackwood. He was born in 1803 at Old Kilpatrick, on the Clyde. By 1826, he had commanded the steam packet *Ayr,* sailing regularly between Glasgow and Ayr, by way of Greenock and Largs. Sometime in the next four years he gave up sailing to become harbourmaster at Ayr, a post he held for most of the 1830s. He had married in 1830, so perhaps a more settled life seemed appropriate. In 1840, however, he became chief officer of the RMS *Britannia,* for her maiden voyage across the Atlantic. Before setting sail, the *Britannia* was one of those ships which had gathered in Leith harbour for the launch of the *Forth.* It is possible that it was there that Blackwood first came in contact with the HLSPC and was attracted to working with them. It certainly seems that transatlantic sailing was not for him, as his obituary records that, after the *Britannia* voyage, he returned to the coastal trade from Glasgow. With four children all under ten, perhaps long voyages did not fit well with family life. Whatever the background, on 30 June 1842 the Company's sailing notices listed Alexander Blackwood as captain of the *Glenalbyn,* and stated that her previous captain, John Brown, would take charge of the new iron vessel then being built. Notices to this effect continued throughout July and August, latterly naming the new ship as the *Martello,* and stating that she would be launched in a few weeks.

The summer board meeting of the Company took place on 1 August 1842, those present being Thomas Barclay, Robert Cook, and Henry Stead and John McKay on behalf of Thompson, McKay. The main business was to find a replacement for Mr Langskill. Eleven applications had been received for the post, and after what was minuted as a 'tedious discussion' it was agreed that the post should be offered to the Company's clerk, John Inkster, at a salary of £100 per annum, and, anticipating an increase in business, to promote William Pringle to First Clerk at an initial annual salary of £80, increasing over two years to £100. There followed arrangements to reinsure both the *Pegasus* and the *Glenalbyn* at

£2,000 each. It was now that the name *Martello* was chosen for the new ship, and arrangements were made to pay Wingate's the third instalment for it. Although details are not given, it is evident that there was also a problem. Captain Brown was selling his shares back to the Company. As his name ceases to appear on sailing notices after the end of August 1842, it seems that he had resigned from his post. Why he decided to quit at this time is a puzzle. To be in at the development of a brand-new cutting-edge ship, and to have been offered its captaincy should have been a captain's dream. What had gone wrong?

» At previous board meetings, John Brown had always been ready to argue his case, and it may be that he showed too much independence for other members of the board.
» Was the decision to leave the *Glenalbyn* to monitor the building of the *Martello* wished upon him rather than his choice?
» Perhaps John Brown was simply a man who liked new challenges.

Whatever the reason, when John Brown's name next appears in listed sailings, it is on 19 August 1842, as Captain of the *Manchester*, a steam ship on the Hull/Hamburg route, landing a mixed cargo, including wool, butter, cigars, leeches and calves at Hull. He moved his family south to Hull, and was to spend the next decade of his life sailing for the Hanseatic Steam Ship Company between the two ports, even having his ship requisitioned for a year by the German Navy in 1847. He was a popular captain. In January 1846, he was presented with a superb silver snuffbox, by the officers under his command, as a testimonial of the high esteem they entertained for the urbanity and kindness universally experienced from him. (*Hull Advertiser and Exchange Gazette* 2 January 1846).

It seems probable that the decision to advertise both the *Pegasus* and the *Glenalbyn* for sale, was also taken at the quarterly meeting. On Saturday, 12 September, the *Shipping and Mercantile Gazette* carried the following advertisement on its front page:

LEITH – THE well-known sea-going Steam-packet PEGASUS, of 130 tons register (exclusive of engine-room) and 120-horse power, elegantly fitted for passengers, and a great carrier, at a fair speed on a light draught of water, at small expense: remarkable for having kept the sea all the memorable hard weather on the east coast these five years past.

Or, the GLENALBYN, of the same tonnage and power, an equally serviceable vessel, chartered in 1840 to carry H.M.'s mail betwixt Hull and Gothenburg, fit for any goods and passenger station her size may suit.

They may be seen every week at Hull and at Leith, betwixt which ports they now ply. Either could be delivered to a purchaser on a short notice.

Apply to the Hull and Leith Steam-packet Company here; T. Barclay, 57 York-street, Glasgow; or to Thompson, McKay, and Co., Hull and Manchester.

JOHN INKSTER.

Leith, August, 1842.

The long-awaited launch of the *Martello* took place on 24 October. It was reported quite fully in the *Caledonian Mercury* 27 October 1842.

Monday, the new steamer built for the Hull and Leith Steam Packet Company, was launched from Messrs Thomas Wingate & Co.'s building yard, Broomielaw, Glasgow, … She is of a very fine model, and a most substantially built ship, having had the advantage of being draughted by Mr Denny, marine architect, with several improvements his experience has been able to suggest in that new and rising branch of shipbuilding, and finished throughout by Messrs Wingate & Co., their sixth iron boat, but the largest they have yet built. This vessel is of the full size of the Liverpool steam packets, and from her fine proportions, is expected to rank with them in their far-famed speed and sea-going properties. She will be a decided improvement on the present traders between Hull and Leith, and form a great attraction to the merchants of Edinburgh and Leith to visit the English markets by a conveyance from their own doors. She will be of the largest dimensions going into Hull docks, and is expected to make the sea part of the passage (from the Bass Rock to Spurn Point) in fifteen hours. The ceremony of naming the packet 'Martello,' was ably performed by Miss Wingate, the daughter of the scientific builder, as she glided majestically into the water.

Among the spectators was Archduke Frederick Ferdinand Leopold of Austria and his party, who were on a state visit to Britain, and had come to Glasgow to look at the city's industrial development.

The final board meeting for 1842, was held on 11 November, but only Thomas Barclay and John Inkster were present. Mr Inkster reported that, in terms of sailings, the last quarter had been uneventful. Financially, a payment of £1,500 to Wingate's had meant that the Company had drawn £970 from the £2,000 credit which the Edinburgh and Leith Bank had made available to them. The sale advertisement for the two ships had produced no purchasers. Several offers to charter one or other of them had been made, but these had been declined. Decisions about a date for the *Martello* to enter service, who would captain her, and who would buy the shares of the late Mr Langskill were deferred, to be discussed by letter with Mr McKay and Captain Cook. Either at the meeting, or subsequently by letter, it was also agreed to extend the fire insurance on the *Pegasus,* as there is a North British Insurance Office receipt dated 26 December, for the payment of five guineas, with 20% duty for £1,000 cover.

On Monday 12 December, the *Martello* made her third sea trial. (The two earlier ones are not recorded). Much of the newspaper coverage of this event concentrated on the ship's fittings, which will be dealt with in a later chapter, but the account of the actual trial, taken from the *Caledonian Mercury* of 15 December 1842, is as follows:

The Martello left the Broomielaw about eight o'clock on Monday morning. This was the third time her steam had been up, and the object of the present trip was to prove her speed where the sea-going packets on the Clyde are always tested, viz. between Greenock quay and Cumbrae Lighthouse. She reached Greenock exactly at sixteen minutes past ten, and the Cumbrae Lighthouse within three minutes and a half of twelve o'clock–having sailed at the rate of thirteen miles an hour, and that, too, against a reefedtop-sail breeze. This, however, although excellent sailing, was not exactly so much as was expected from her. This was owing to a defect in one of the engine valves, which is immediately to be remedied. After reaching the Cumbrae Lighthouse, the next object was to try how she would breast the waves of the ocean beyond that point, where the sea usually rolls in with great power, and on that day particularly so; and for this purpose her sail was prolonged for seven or eight miles farther. The result, we are glad to say, was highly satisfactory, and proved her to be in every respect worthy of confidence. On her return she made the trip between Cumbrae and Greenock five minutes sooner than before, and arrived at the Broomielaw about half-past four o'clock.

It must have been a satisfying end to the year for Thomas Barclay and the Company, perhaps less reassuring for the crews of the existing ships.

CHAPTER 10

SAILINGS DURING 1842

The year began as the old year had ended – the *Pegasus* was still undergoing repair in Hull, and the service between Leith and Hull had been reduced to a weekly one, with the *Glenalbyn*, commanded by John Brown, sailing from Leith each Wednesday and returning from Hull on Saturdays. The *Pegasus* finally resumed service on 12 February 1842, and, in an effort to boost her now somewhat tarnished reputation, the Company ordered 2,200 fliers to advertise 'The Return of the *Pegasus*'. As soon as she was on post, the *Glenalbyn* was withdrawn for her winter overhaul. This was intended to be a much shorter affair, described in advertisements as for 'a few days' but in fact the service took exactly a month. In an advertisement for the beginning of their joint sailings, on 12 March 1842, both ships were described as in 'the highest state of efficiency'. The actual sailings for both ships seem to have been largely uneventful throughout the year, but problems, many of which ended up in court, were caused by cargoes, crew and passengers, particularly for the *Pegasus*.

When the *Pegasus* sailed from Leith on 12 March, in her cargo were two casks of oil, for delivery to Thompson, McKay, for onward transportation. These were unloaded at Hull on 14 March and left at the end of the Humber Dock. Sometime between then and Saturday 19 March, one of the casks was stolen. On the Saturday evening, a labourer, James Ayre, attempted to sell a barrel of oil. From the report of the Magistrates' Court, it would appear that getting rid of the barrel was not as easy as presumably he had thought. During the evening, he was seen in the taproom of the *Commercial Hotel*, where he claimed he was delivering two casks to Spyvee & Cooper, the rope and twine merchants in Lime Street. Clearly this did not work, as he subsequently tried to sell the barrel to a John Richardson, claiming he had been given it by John Ashton, who was known locally as a thief. Richardson was not interested but suggested he take it to the cooper, John Tadman. Tadman offered him half a crown for the oil, to be paid on delivery the following Monday. The cooper, however, was not as gullible as he first appeared, and on Ayre leaving, he contacted Thompson, McKay and discovered that they had lost one of their barrels. So it was that when Ayre returned to collect his money on Monday, he was arrested, and brought before the magistrates the following day, together with John Ashton, the man Ayre claimed had stolen the barrel. William Beckett, a local sailor, confirmed that the barrel in question had been landed from the *Pegasus*.

Ayre said that Ashton had called him out of the pub to ask him to sell the barrel but could produce no evidence to back up his claim. Ralph Dry, who had been in the taproom on Saturday night, contradicted this account by saying that Ashton had been in the pub, and only later did Ayre come in. That evidence, probably helped by the fact that, unlike Ayre, Ashton was represented by a lawyer, resulted in the case against Ashton being dismissed, but Ayre was committed for trial. The trial took place on 22 June, when Ayre was found guilty of 'larceny from a wharf', and sentenced to four months imprisonment. The thief had been caught and punished, but one is left wondering why the barrels were left lying on the dockside in the first place. Was it neglect on the part of the *Pegasus*, or by the shipping agents, or more likely, was it standard practice to leave goods on the quayside until they were ready to be loaded on to the next ship?

The *Pegasus* may have been incidental to the case of the stolen barrel, but at the end of the month, she featured directly in a case of smuggling. She sailed from Leith on the afternoon of Saturday, 26 March 1842. She docked at Hull late on the Sunday. On the

Monday morning, the ship's mate, Benjamin Beaumont, arranged for a dock labourer, George Grayburn, to come on board to collect a bag of dirty linen, presumably to take it to the laundry. About midday, Grayburn left the ship carrying the bag, only to be followed by Mr Jones, a customs officer, who, it seemed, had been advised to watch for people disembarking from the *Pegasus*. After a little, he stopped Grayburn and searched the bag. It did indeed contain dirty clothing, but hidden within it was a gallon bottle containing seven and a half pints of whisky! Grayburn denied absolutely that the whisky was anything to do with him, saying that the mate had simply asked him to carry the bag of laundry. A gallon bottle of whisky was a serious issue. Scotch whisky carried a duty of seven shillings and ten pence per gallon, but it was illegal to import it into England in quantities of less than twenty-five gallons – so concealing and moving a single gallon could only be case of smuggling. Grayburn was arrested, and Beaumont was called in for questioning. The first the company knew of the matter was when Thompson, McKay sent a brief note, dated 1 April 1842, to James Langskill by way of Captain Brown on the *Glenalbyn*, to say that Captain Miller would inform them of the mate's smuggling.

The case came before the Hull magistrates on Tuesday, 19 April. George Grayburn, who was defended by a Mr Johnson, again claimed that he had merely agreed to carry the bag and knew nothing of the whisky. Mr Johnson attempted to confuse matters by asking if the customs officer was sure it was Scotch and not Irish whiskey. The officer conceded that he could not tell the difference, but since the bottle had definitely come from the *Pegasus*, he was sure this was Scotch. Beaumont was then called to give evidence. He stated that Grayburn was not a crew member, but a labourer who had been asked to move the dirty linen, and that Grayburn did not know that the bag contained whisky. When asked how the whisky came to be in the bag, he refused to answer lest he incriminate himself. This left the court with a dilemma – it seemed to be clear to all present that the true smuggler was Beaumont, but they had no actual evidence of this. Whisky had been smuggled and Grayburn had been found with it, so he must be found guilty.

A further complication was that the legislation relating to the smuggling of spirits was confusing. Under an 1828 Statute of George IV, the penalty for such smuggling was between £100 and £25 – even at its lowest, well and beyond what a labourer could pay. Mr Johnson, the solicitor drew attention to a more recent law passed in 1831, in the reign of William IV, which set the minimum fine in relation to smuggled spirits at £5. This, however, was declared inadmissible, as it applied only to *foreign* spirits, and whisky coming from Scotland could not be considered foreign! Grayburn was fined £25 and imprisoned for three months, since he could not pay. Unusually, the magistrates concluded the case with a statement in support of Grayburn, and highly critical of Beaumont:

> They could see no power they possessed of mitigating the penalty lower than £25. The case was hard upon the prisoner, the mate being the offending party, who ought to pay the fine. They felt exceedingly the hardship of the case, and would be glad to sign any memorial for the release of the prisoner from confinement.
>
> From accounts in Hull newspapers 22 April 1842

If the magistrates could see no way of dealing with Beaumont, the Company had no such problems. Beaumont was sacked immediately when the result of the trial reached the board.

As if two court cases were not enough, before April was over, the *Pegasus* was also involved in a coroner's inquest, following the death of a passenger on board. On Monday, 18 April 1842, at the *Wellington Tavern* in Hull, both the master, Alexander Miller, and the second mate, Thomas Miller, were required to give evidence into the death of Joshua Mortimer. The incident had begun on Saturday, 16 April. Mortimer was one of the passengers joining the ship in Leith that day. He was a wool dyer from Heckmondwike in the West Riding of Yorkshire. According to the crew, when Mr Mortimer came on board, he was already tipsy. Mortimer had been born in Dewsbury, but as a young man, had moved to Bannockburn, by Stirling, where he lived with his family for about the next fifteen years. Almost certainly he was employed at the mills of Wilsons of Bannockburn, at that time one of the foremost tartan weaving companies in Scotland. In such a place, Mortimer's wool dyeing skills would be highly prized. Presumably, it was also during these years that he became addicted to whisky, an addiction which probably cost him his job and resulted in the move back to the West Riding – he was certainly living there in 1841. Once on board the *Pegasus*, Mortimer demanded more whisky, but it was agreed not to serve him any. Thomas Miller gave evidence at the inquest that, about seven p.m. on the Saturday, he and one of the cabin boys had helped Mortimer to the deck, he being tipsy and having been sick. At midnight, the mate saw him again, lying on the deck. At five a.m. he was still there, though somehow he had found, or been given, a pillow of straw.

At this point Miller and the other mate covered him with their jackets. Two hours later, as there was no sign of his waking, they moved him into a side room off the deck. From then until his death, about five p.m., Mortimer neither spoke nor opened his eyes. Alexander Miller told the inquest that, on seeing him on the Sunday morning, he had ordered that his temples should be bathed with cold water, which was done several times during the day. This intervention, however, came too late. As the *Pegasus* approached Spurn Point, about five p.m. on the Sunday, Mortimer had a serious stroke and died almost immediately. Both the master and the mate had believed that Mortimer was simply drunk. As it was a sudden death, with no trained medical men to witness it, an inquest was necessary after the ship docked in Hull. Evidence was given that Mortimer had died from an effusion of blood on the brain. The jury's verdict was 'Died by the visitation of God'.

The ongoing references to the *Pegasus* in these cases, cannot have helped her reputation, although, apart from a dishonest mate, none of them were actually the fault of the ship. It must therefore have come as a relief to receive rather different attention in the newspapers in April. At the beginning of the month, the rail service between Hull and London had lowered its fares, thereby reducing the cost of through journeys from Scotland to the capital. This was a matter of interest as far north as John o' Groats, where on 8 April, the *John o' Groat Journal* published the details under the heading:

> NOTHING LIKE STEAM – We are now able to make the same boast as our American friends, 'that it is as cheap to travel as to stay at home!' That we are entitled to do so, we will state, that a man can now travel to London from this place, for 28s.! The 'Sovereign,' steamer, will take him to Leith for 18s.; from thence he can travel, by the 'Pegasus,' to Hull for 7s.6d.; and from thence to London, for 2s.6d.!!! Who would not, now, take a trip to 'the great metropolis?' We may mention, as a contrast to the above, that, by the mail-coach it would cost £10 18s.

Once published in the *Journal*, the article was taken up and republished by other newspapers across the country, bringing much needed positive publicity for the *Pegasus*.

Following the Company's appointment of Alexander Blackwood as a captain for their fleet, his first sailing on the *Glenalbyn* from Leith to Hull took place on 15 June 1842.

At the end of August 1842, the case of the wool which had been brought to Hull in September 1841, and kept in storage there, finally came to court at Leeds. The long delay had been due to doubt as to who had a claim on the wool after Samuel Eastwood's bankruptcy. Initially it had seemed that the wool bales were either still the property of Adam & Russell, the wool merchants at Bonnington, who had never received payment for them, or to the assignees who had been appointed on behalf of Eastwood's creditors. At the end of 1841, this had finally been resolved in favour of Adam and Russell, but when they had attempted to reclaim their goods from the wharfinger, Jesse Malcolm, at Hull, he refused to release them. His case was that he was due payment from Eastwood for the storage of the goods, and as Eastwood could not pay him, he was entitled to keep the bales himself in lieu of payment. Again, the *Glenalbyn* and the *Pegasus* were named in the considerable newspaper coverage of the case, as ships which had helped bring the consignment, although, in fact, the actual bales in store had been brought to Hull by a third ship, the *John Watson*. The evidence, as presented, did not show Malcolm in a particularly good light, as he had said nothing about his interests until the wool merchants actually arrived to collect their wool at the end of December. At this time, rather than discussing the matter with them, Malcolm had refused to release the wool, and told them to go and see his solicitor. It then took another seven months to come to court. After all the evidence was heard, the court found in favour of Adam and Russell, and awarded them £378.12s.2d damages.

In early September, there must have been some excitement among the crews of both the *Pegasus* and the *Glenalbyn*, when they found themselves carrying horses for the famous St. Leger Race at Doncaster. On 7 September 1842, the *Glenalbyn* carried 'three celebrated horses', which, when landed at Hull, were refreshed at Bonsell's Livery Stables in Carr Lane, and then sent on by train to Doncaster. The following weekend, the *Pegasus* brought a racehorse named *Triumph*, another horse and a filly, all of which were fed and watered at the *Vittoria Hotel* by the pier, before travelling on by train for the races. Did the crew have a flutter on the horses they had carried? If so, those on the *Pegasus* seem likely to have been disappointed – no trace can be found of a horse called *Triumph* running in any of the races – perhaps the sea journey had not agreed with him/her. It is possible that the *Glenalbyn* crew may have been luckier – that year the St. Leger was won by a Scottish filly – the Earl of Eglinton's *Blue Bonnet*, though there is no way of being sure that she had been on the *Glenalbyn*.

The last months of the year seem to have been uneventful. There are very few advertisements for the sailings – perhaps a deliberate saving, seeing that, as a result of the costs of building the *Martello*, the company was overdrawn at the bank; nor are there any reports of cargoes or incidents in relation to either ship. We do know, however, that the service was still running, thanks to reports from the Marine Telegraph. The telegraph was the brainchild of Barnard Lindsay Watson – a lieutenant in the West Oxford Militia, and was originally developed for the Liverpool Dock Trustees as:

> … a speedy Mode of Communication to the Ship-owners and Merchants at Liverpool of the Port of Liverpool or the Coast of Wales, by building, erecting and maintaining Signal Houses, Telegraphs or other such Modes of Communication as shall seem to them expedient …
>
> 6 Geo IV clxxxvii

The system proved a great success, and Watson added to it by producing a manual and sets of signalling flags to allow ships to communicate with the signal houses and with each other.

In March 1839, the Hull Chamber of Commerce had commissioned Watson to set up a semaphore telegraph system connecting Hull with Grimsby and Spurn Head, to report the arrival of ships from Northern Europe, and by using flags to communicate with them. The following year, Watson created an umbrella body for these developments – the General Telegraph Association and created a series of stations round the British coast. In relation to the Company's ships, the building of one at Flamborough Head was relevant. Each registered ship was given a unique number, and instructions to fly flags and/or pennants indicating that number, which could then be read from the signal station and duly recorded. If necessary, the full set of flags could be used by the ships to send messages to the station or other passing ships. The *Pegasus* was number 2170, and the *Glenalbyn* number 2303. Some of their movements for the latter months of 1842 can be tracked from the pages of the *Shipping and Mercantile Gazette* which reported the telegraph messages from the Flamborough Head station.

DATE	SHIP	TIME	TRAVEL	CONDITIONS
16 Oct. 1842	*Pegasus*	10.15 am	Leith/Hull	Wind N., light breezes
3 Nov. 1842	*Glenalbyn*	2.00 am	Leith/Hull	Wind E. to E.S.E., light breezes, hazy
13 Nov. 1842	*Pegasus*	11.00 am	Leith/Hull	Wind S.W.
25 Dec. 1842	*Pegasus*	4.15 pm	Leith/Hull	Wind S.W., strong breezes

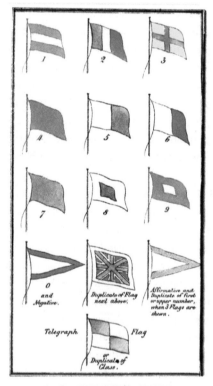

CODE OF TELEGRAPH SIGNALS.

London: Published by Henry Kent Causton & Cº Birchin Lane.

Watson's Signal Code from The Handbook of Communication by Telegraph 1842

CHAPTER 11

THE *MARTELLO* ENTERS SERVICE

The new year began with both the *Glenalbyn* and the *Pegasus* on station. Returning to Leith from Hull, on 2 January, the *Glenalbyn* was forced to take shelter from a storm in Bridlington Bay. She reached Leith, however, without damage. There, she took on board a very unusual cargo – a number of new stagecoaches for use in the Yorkshire and Lincolnshire area. These had been built in Perth by Patrick Wallace, who had been supplying the Royal Mail with coaches for Scotland since 1835. In 1842 he had been awarded a seven-year contract to supply coaches throughout the kingdom, and also a Royal Warrant as 'Her Majesty's Coachbuilder for Scotland', though the large part Wallace had played in decorating Perth for the 1842 Royal Visit, may also have contributed to the granting of the warrant. Taking the coaches to Hull was to be the first leg of the *Glenalbyn's* last voyage on the route for the time being, as she was withdrawn from service on 7 January 1843.

Meanwhile, the *Martello* was being prepared to go into service. A Company advertisement on 11 January 1843, stated that the *Martello* would sail from Glasgow for Leith on Saturday 14 January, by way of the Pentland Firth.

> This NEW STEAM-PACKET, the second this Company have built expressly for this Trade, is as large as very sanguine expectations of an increase of public support alone could warrant, and so powerful as to put her speed in all weathers on a par with the very best Steam-Packets of the present day. No pains or expense has been spared in her Hull, Engines, Cabins, or Equipments, to make her in every respect worthy to occupy

the great thoroughfare from the Capital of Scotland to Hull, the entrepôt of the Continent of Europe, and the affluent Midland Counties and Manufacturing Districts of England.

The Scotsman 11 January 1843

Not a Company to miss a trick, they aimed to make the necessary voyage profitable, advertising in the *John o' Groat Journal* of 13 January 1843:

STEAM TRIP FROM THURSO AND WICK TO LEITH. – The splendid and large new steamer 'Martello' for the Hull and Leith trade, built at Glasgow, in going to her destination, sails from Glasgow, on the 14th to call at Scrabster Roads, Thurso, and Wick, on the 16th, when she will proceed direct to Leith from thence. Passengers going south at this season cannot get so commodious a conveyance anywhere. And we are certain that the curious and scientific persons in Caithness, including sections of the fair sex, will find something worth inspecting in this powerful, and, expected to be, fast vessel, which is entirely built of iron.

It was a measure of how much merchant shipping had improved in the seven years since the *Pegasus* had made the same journey, that no mention was made of any difficulties in sailing through the Pentland Firth.

The ship which came into harbour at Leith, was certainly very splendid, and clearly the Company had spared no effort to ensure that their vessel was of the highest quality, although, with a canny eye to cost, the men who had been chosen to create the *Martello* were all professionals still making their name, rather than established stars. William Denny, the ship's designer, was only twenty-seven, but would go on to found the Denny Brothers Shipbuilding Company, the builders of many famous ships over the next century, including the *Cutty Sark*. James Rochead, who was responsible for the interior design of the *Martello*, had set up his architect's practice only two years previously, but later in his career, would win the competition to build the Wallace Monument on the edge of Stirling. The actual fitting out of the interior was entrusted to the long-established Glasgow firm of Alexander Fotheringham, cabinet makers, upholsterers and wood merchants, while the painted decorations were the work of another up-and-coming craftsman, the artist, J. Mylne. The work of these men was the icing on the *Martello's* cake. The main saloon was fitted out in Elizabethan style with panelled oak and elaborate carvings. In the entrance area a series of spiral columns were separated by framed mirrors, above which was a panelled ceiling decorated in the style of the Spanish Alhambra. At the centre was a glass cupola on which were the coats of arms of the Scottish and English cities whose trade the new ship would support. Fixed seating and sofas were covered in rich figured crimson plush. The separate Ladies' Cabin had a number of individual berths, each fitted with pierced panels lined with crimson silk damask. Spacious and well lighted accommodation had also been provided for the steerage passengers below deck, and, as the contemporary accounts say, the good ventilation system was of particular interest to the passengers.

Once on station, the *Martello*, commanded by Alexander Blackwood, made her first sailing to Hull on Saturday 21 January 1843. Travelling through poor weather, she reached Hull in 20½ hours, reducing the average time for the voyage by some six hours. The piers were packed with sightseers to watch her arrival. Once docked, and passengers and cargo disembarked, the *Martello* became the centre of a marketing campaign. Members of the board had travelled down on her, and, with the captain, they proceeded to conduct the curious over the ship, answering questions, and pointing out significant features, according to the particular interests of the visitors. Then, on the Wednesday morning, prior to leaving for Leith, a large group of specially invited guests were taken on an excursion sail up the River Humber. She left the docks for Leith about three in the afternoon, to the cheers of a large crowd which had gathered on the piers to see her off.

As soon as the *Martello* had completed her return voyage, advertisements for the Company, while still listing all three ships, made it clear that now the *Pegasus* too, was to be withdrawn from service 'for a short time' following her return from Hull on 19 January 1843. In the following weeks, the *Martello* would sail from Leith on Saturdays and from Hull on Wednesdays. Economically it made sense — winter sailings were never fully subscribed, and since the *Martello* was almost double the size of the other two ships, she could certainly cover demand in a single weekly sailing. Also, this had always been the time when the other ships were serviced. In late January and early February, the Company embarked on a real marketing drive. New arrangements were made for the carriage of goods by rail from Sheffield to Hull, before loading for Leith:

> ... N.B. – Goods, &c. from Sheffield and its Vicinity for the above Vessels, should be in the care of MARY JACKSON, Railway Carrier, the previous Night, by Half-past Six o'Clock at the latest, to Sail as above.
>
> *Sheffield Independent* 7 January 1843

At the same time, the voyages to Leith were advertised in many papers with the strap line:

> Whence there are Daily conveyances to Glasgow, Stirling, the Lochs, and to all places on the East and West of Scotland.

Sailing south, the onward rail connections were listed — as were the times of the train connections:

> Passengers will arrive in Hull in good time for the Evening Railway Train (at 4.55) for London, Leeds, Derby, Birmingham, Sheffield, York, Rochdale, Manchester, &c., &c. ...There are FOUR RAILWAY TRAINS from HULL DAILY – First at 6.25, and Second at 10.30 a.m. and Third at 1.25, and Fourth at 4.55 p.m. Two only on Sunday.

Nevertheless, the fact that the final line of several of these advertisements stated that both the *Glenalbyn* and the *Pegasus* were for sale, must have been a concern for their crews.

Description of the *Martello*

The Martello, we have learned, was built at Glasgow, and is the fifth iron vessel of large dimensions launched into the Clyde. She combines many important adaptions and improvements, of which the progress of that branch of ship-building at Liverpool and Glasgow, together with great practical experience, have suggested the adoption. The easy convertability of malleable iron has enabled her builders to put together a fabric uniting complete strength with scientific modelling for a sea-going boat in a very remarkable manner. Her strong beams and arches, and watertight bulk-heads, must, on examination, give the public a high degree of confidence in the capability of such vessels to resist the influence of any storm, under skilful seamanship. Her engines, which are of 250 horse-power, are the manufacture of those distinguished engineers, Messrs Thomas Wingate and Co., of Spring-field, Glasgow, who also built the vessel; and they afford a very favourable idea of the present advanced state of marine engineering, making, as does the vessel itself of the skill and assiduity of her builders. They are of *direct connexion*, sometimes called vertical engines. It might appear at first sight that the weight of her connecting rods, and their guides, above deck, must have a tendency to make the vessel top heavy, and uneasy, in a seaway; but the engineer explained to us, that the paddle wheels, shafts, and cranks, being in this construction, quite as low set as in any other vessel, the little weight of the malleable iron connecting rods and their guides, in comparison to the massive cast iron cylinders, condensers, air pumps, steam valves, boilers, and other weight below, was quite insignificant, or to quote his own illustration, 'no more than the comparative weight of the feather in a lady's bonnet.' The patent wire rigging, Porter's and Rogers' patent anchors, and her whole deck equipments, all show that no expense has been spared to make her a substantial and durable seaboat.

The model of the Martello—which was draughted by Mr Denny, comprehends some rather remarkable novelties, in round stern, clipper bow, and hurricane deck; and an exceedingly fine entrance and run contribute to make her the very swift and easy vessel her passages have proved her to be.

The interior fittings and arrangements of the Martello are at once unique and commodious. Her cabins are got in the Moorish Alhambra fashion, in a style of splendour and comfort seldom if ever witnessed before. She has eight separate state rooms, besides a spacious and elegant saloon—affording her passengers that sleeping accommodation, combined with ease and privacy, so desireable in a night passage, in unfavourable weather. The elaborate fret-work panels of the doors and sleeping berths, and the gorgeous carved and illuminated work of the roof and cupola, will be a lasting memorial of the talent of the architect, Mr Rochead, of Glasgow. The solid spiral columns, and the fretted chairs or stalls with which the saloon is surrounded, the massive oak tables and other cabinet work, exhibit at once the finest taste and most excellent workmanship. The ceiling is beautifully ornamented in heraldic and illuminated old English designs, by Mr Mylne, a young and rising artist of Glasgow, which give the apartments a very light and elegant appearance. The ladies' cabins, which are also highly decorated, are sufficiently spacious, well fitted up with couches and easy chairs, and have private sleeping apartments attached.

From the *Hull Packet*, 27 January 1843

Description of Martello

On 4 February 1843, the quarterly board meeting, attended by Thomas Barclay and Captain Cook, with John Inkster keeping the minutes, reviewed the position of the three ships. With regard to the *Martello*, so far Wingate's had been paid £8,000, all that was currently due; Fotheringham's had received £900 on account; and there had also been an outlay for chains, anchor ropes, plated goods and crockery, but as other builders' and joiners' accounts were still awaited, the overall cost of the ship could not be calculated. The payments had left the Company overdrawn at the Bank to the tune of £1,175. In line with previous practice, as part of the publicity for the new ship, John Inkster had issued some 650 free tickets to Scottish friends and customers of the Company, and a further 600 had been given out by Messrs Thompson, McKay at the English end. One outstanding item was the installation of a flag for the *Martello* at the Leith Signal Station, provided it could be procured for a guinea!

Leith Signal Station – 1829 print by Thomas Shepherd

The role of the Leith Signal Station, an adapted windmill tower on the foreshore, was used to signal the state of the tide and the water depth to incoming ships. It is not clear why the *Martello* should have needed its own flag, since, if separate flags had been raised for every ship, the building would have looked less like a signal station and more like a washing green! It has been suggested that the *Martello's* larger size and draught possibly required ship-specific instructions to be signalled. Alternatively, in line with a practice common at some other ports, and at a time when strict schedules were not possible, the arrival of a particular passenger and cargo ship could be signalled to the city by raising its flag on the signal station.

Thomas Barclay and Robert Cook seem to have made an executive decision to have the *Glenalbyn* lengthened and otherwise improved. Mr Barclay had been in discussion with William Denny and had obtained plans and a model for lengthening the ship by twenty-six feet forward. The specifications for this work to be done on the Clyde, were to be issued the following week. At the same time, Wingate's had been commissioned to provide a new boiler, to which Symington's patent condensing plan was to be applied – this was a system whereby the condensing of the spent steam was achieved by sending it through a pipe on the outside of the ship, below the water line, after which the water was re-injected into the boiler. As always, Thomas Barclay was keen to make use of the latest technology, and this system, which had been trialled on steamships over the previous three years, had been shown to reduce wear to the boilers, reduce fuel costs by a quarter and increase the speed of the ships.

The *Pegasus* was also to benefit from new technology – in this case, Charles Wye Williams' patent improved furnace, 'warranted to economise both heat and fuel, and to prevent smoke, by effecting a perfect chemical combustion of the fuel'. Charles Williams was a highly inventive entrepreneur with interests in several fields, Managing Director of the City of Dublin Steam Packet Company, and, in 1837, one of the founders of the Peninsular and Orient Line, now more commonly known as P. & O. Having successfully used the system on his own ships, he was now making it available to other companies. In February 1843, one of his men had come over from Dublin to Leith and was in the process of fitting the new type of furnace to the *Pegasus*. The actual cost of this alteration is not recorded, but the Company did have to pay eight shillings and sixpence for the freight of the furnace doors and other related items.

With both the *Pegasus* and the *Glenalbyn* undergoing modifications, it was agreed that the *Martello* alone would cover the Leith/Hull route until the end of March, unless a second boat was needed sooner. Both the *Pegasus* and the *Glenalbyn* were to remain offered for sale, but when the summer season began, it was intended that the *Pegasus* would become the second vessel on the route. The longer-term future of the *Glenalbyn* was not mentioned. The final business of the meeting was a discussion of freight charges – several customers had applied for the charges to be reduced, but after discussion, it was agreed that the current prices should be maintained.

There must have been an increased demand during the spring, for, despite what had been agreed, the *Pegasus* was listed to sail from Leith to Hull on Wednesday, 22 March 1843. Before this, however, there was a trial sail on the River Forth, on Saturday 18 March, to test the new Williams' modifications. This was reported in the *Caledonian Mercury* of 23 March:

> On Saturday, the Pegasus steamer made a trial trip, from Leith round Inchkeith, to prove the working of Mr Williams's patent furnace, for saving fuel and consuming smoke, ... The trial was very satisfactory indeed, there being a full supply of steam at seven pounds of pressure even while the vessel was light, and the engine running away betwixt twenty-four and twenty-five revolutions in a minute. The usual blackness of the smoke was considerably reduced; and this particular will be entirely effected when the firemen have more experience in regulating the draught. One voyage or two will suffice for this; and it is

confidently expected, from this short run, that a very great saving will be made in the fuel used in a voyage.

On 22 March 1843, the journey south was uneventful, but on her return from Hull there were problems. Off St Abb's Head, on Sunday, 26 March, the *Pegasus* ran into a severe storm, as a result of which the centre of one of her paddle wheels was broken. Despite *The Scotsman*, reporting that this incident had not impeded her progress, it was not until one p.m. on the Monday afternoon that she limped into Leith, almost twenty-four hours after she was due. Initially it was thought that the mishap was slight, and she was withdrawn from service for a week for repairs. The damage, however, proved to be greater than anticipated, and a new shaft, crank and iron block had to be ordered and brought by train from Glasgow. She did not sail again from Leith until 15 April 1843.

No mention of the accident was made at the next board meeting on 6 May 1843. Mr Inkster reported that the steamers generally had had a good spring trade, but that goods traffic was now lessening, as was usual in the late spring. Thomas Barclay was concerned about the unevenness of traffic on the two ships – and referred to the crowded state of the *Martello's* cabin, in contrast to only two or three cabin passengers on the *Pegasus*. Mr Inkster was instructed to write to Thompson, McKay with a view to reducing passenger fares on the *Pegasus* and improving uptake. It is not recorded whether this letter was written, but certainly there were no alterations to the fares for the *Pegasus* up until her last voyage on 19 July 1843.

Settling the final accounts for the *Martello* was proving difficult, and the Company was in dispute with both Wingate's and Fotheringham about what was still owing. In both instances, however, steps had been taken to secure referees to agree the issues, if it did not prove possible to settle matters amicably. The alterations to the *Glenalbyn* were still ongoing – the ship had been replanked and the boilers were being installed, but progress had been slower than expected.

May 1843 was an uneventful month for the ships on the route, but in June both were carrying Scots 'well-fed cattle' to Hull for the English markets – sixteen on the *Pegasus* on 14 June, and a further ten on the *Martello* on 17 June. A listing of cargo for the *Martello*, from Hull to Leith survives for the sailing on 19 July – four cases of machinery, six casks of oil, twenty-three barrels of resin, eight sheets of wool, seventy bars of iron and seventy-seven miscellaneous packages.

By the end of June 1843, it seems as if the ongoing work on the *Glenalbyn* had been completed, and local newspapers carried advertisements for her setting sail from Glasgow for Leith at two p.m. on 17 July 1843. As had been done with the *Martello* earlier in the year, the voyage to her home port was to be combined with tourist excursions en route:

> She will, weather permitting, make a TOUR of STAFFA and IONA, STORNOWAY, the KYLES of SKYE, THURSO, and other interesting places in the WEST and NORTH HIGHLANDS. ...

> Such an opportunity of visiting the distant romantic Scenery of the West and North Highlands is rarely to be met with, – both on account of the speed of the vessel and the moderate fare.

The full voyage was to cost three guineas. When the date for sailing arrived, however, the newspapers carried a note of its postponement, as further testing of her engines and boilers was required. The planned tour was now scheduled for 31 July 1843.

All seemed set fair for a good summer season for the Company, but that was not to be.

PART 2

THE TRAGEDY AND ITS AFTERMATH

PART 2

CHAPTER 12

FINAL VOYAGE

When the *Pegasus* left Leith for Hull sometime after five p.m., on Wednesday 19 July 1843, as far as is known, there was aboard a crew of sixteen, forty-one booked passengers (eighteen cabin and twenty-three steerage). Booked passengers collected their tickets from the Company's office on the quayside. Additional passengers who came on board on the Wednesday afternoon were not recorded. The arrangement was that, once on board, the mate collected the purchased tickets, and money from those without tickets. As a result, there was no definitive list of all those who sailed with the *Pegasus* that afternoon. One group of late joiners included a small group of soldiers – possibly a Captain O'Neil, a Sergeant Mackay or Munro, and others. They did not have travel warrants and were thought to be men on leave. They attracted attention as the sergeant, who was somewhat drunk, tried to get the captain to agree to provide a cabin place at a steerage fare, for the pregnant wife of another sergeant. When the captain would not agree, Mackay/Munro became obstreperous, and the Company's clerk was summoned. The group remained on board, but no special arrangements were recorded. It was only the altercation over the cabin which led to their presence on board being noted. How many other late additions there were remains unknown. One group of army recruits arrived at the harbour, only to see the *Pegasus* sailing out into the Forth.

The ship's crew were the captain, Alexander Miller; first mate, William Brown; second mate, Thomas Miller, brother of the captain; engineers, William Hood and Alexander Agnew; firemen, Daniel Campbell, William Knaresborough and William

McCoombs; sailors, Robert Melville and John (Jack) Johnstone (or Johnson); ship's apprentice, Andrew Dowie or Dowely; carpenter, George Taylor; ship's cook, Robert Marshall; and stewards, George Parker and Louisa Howard.

As always on forms of public transport, the passengers came from a wide variety of backgrounds[9] and were on the ship for many different reasons. The most famous by far was Mr William Elton, a celebrated Shakespearean actor, returning south for further engagements, after performing at the *Adelphi Theatre*, Edinburgh, in *Richard III*, and *Anthony and Cleopatra*, as well as other now less well-known plays. Another distinguished passenger was the Reverend John Morell Mackenzie, a lecturer at Glasgow's Congregational Theological College, who was travelling south to visit his sister and parents, after spending a short holiday at Portobello with his wife. He had deliberately chosen to go by the *Pegasus* rather than the *Martello*, to avoid travelling on the Sabbath. Among the rest were:

» Thomas Hodgson (26), a young man who had been visiting his parents in Edinburgh, and doubtless celebrating his good fortune, before taking up a new post as Assistant Secretary to the Leeds Mechanics' Institution and Literary Society.
» Two boys off on their holidays, Master Elliott (6), from Dundee, was accompanying his uncle, James, a solicitor, to his home in Rochdale; David Scott (11), the son of a Paisley shawl manufacturer was being taken to London by his old nurse, Mrs Stewart.
» A group of young people, travelling back to Lincolnshire – Fanny Flowers (11) was the daughter of the Rector of Tealby, going home for a delayed summer holiday, as she had caught measles and had to remain at Miss Banks' boarding school in

---

9 A full list of identified passengers together with what is known of them is given in the appendix.

Edinburgh for the first weeks of the holiday; with her was another lady from the boarding school, Isabella Hopton (30)[10], also Fanny's brother Field (13), who, with a family friend, Maria Barton (26) from nearby Market Rasen, had travelled to Edinburgh to see the sights, visit the school and accompany Fanny home.

» Charles Bailey (39), a former sailor and ferryman, on the ship as a companion to Robinson Torry (27), a young draper's apprentice from Market Rasen, who seems to have suffered some form of breakdown, and had been travelling for his health.

» William Primrose (22), a young man, returning from Glasgow, where he had married his pregnant sweetheart. He was now on his way to his employment as a stonemason at Stoke Rochford Hall in Lincolnshire.

» Robert Hildyard (23), a sailor, the son of a Curate of Beverley Minster.

» William Milne (c.27), the son of the Edinburgh shoemaker to the Queen. William was travelling to London to widen his experience of business.

» Arthur Moxham (23), a Glamorgan man who had been on a tour of the Highlands with his brother Egbert, who lived in Edinburgh.

» There were also a number of soldiers, some apparently en route to India. One group was a recruiting party of the 96th Regiment consisting of Lance-Sergeant William Scotter, Corporal B. Dunn, Private J. Harford and Private R. Liddell, together with a recruit for the 78th Regiment, J. McDougal, and the Lance Sergeant's wife, Martha, and son, John, a boy of seven. With them travelled Susan Allan, a young girl who was going out to India to join her father, a soldier in the 25th Regiment.

---

10 Accounts generally describe her as Fanny's school friend, but census records suggest she was considerably older, possibly a teacher or companion assigned to Fanny by the school. One account gives her destination as Market Rasen, so perhaps she was actually Maria Barton's friend.

The story of what happened on this fateful voyage is mainly drawn from the accounts given by five of the six survivors – William Brown, first mate, William Hood, ship's engineer, Daniel Campbell, fireman, and the passengers, Charles Bailey and Robert Hildyard. It had been a fine summer's day in Edinburgh, and the ship set sail on a calm evening, possibly a little hazy, but nothing to cause concern. Egbert Moxham stood on the quay, waving his brother off, until he was no longer visible. It must have been pleasant on board the ship. Morell Mackenzie remained on deck watching the coastline until St. Abb's Head was passed, then retired to bed just after ten p.m. Charles Bailey saw his charge to his cabin, and then at about seven-thirty p.m., met with Captain Miller, whom he knew from previous voyages, and took tea with him in the captain's cabin, before joining other passengers on the deck to enjoy the evening sun. At about ten-thirty p.m., people in Berwick, walking on the town ramparts, coincidentally after watching a tented performance of Mr Van Amburgh's *Menagerie*, saw the ship steam south. In Berwick Bay, she encountered part of the herring fishing fleet, and may have changed course to avoid the nets. At about eleven forty-five p.m., the *Pegasus* passed the white pyramid marker on Emmanuel Head, the easternmost point of Holy Island, and the lights on the Farne Islands were clearly visible then. From there, following her usual route, she headed towards the Inner Passage. By now, everyone had retired except the crew on duty. At midnight, eight bells were rung, signalling crew changes. The captain went to the bridge. Daniel Campbell, the fireman, relieved of his duties, came on deck for some fresh air; Jack Johnstone, the helmsman, handed the wheel over to Robert Melville, and, on his way back to his bunk, wakened William Brown, the mate. The normal arrangement was that Thomas Miller, the second mate, roused Brown to take his place, but on this evening, the second mate had not appeared. As a result, William was late on duty. Then, at about twelve-twenty a.m., the ship, powered by both engine and sails, struck a submerged reef at speed. This proved to be the Goldstone Rock, a known hazard on this stretch of the coastal route. For some reason, the *Pegasus* was half a mile to the east of her normal route.

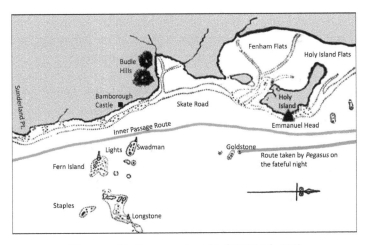

The route of the Pegasus on the night of 19/20 July 1843
Based on Kelso and Berwick Warder 19 August 1843

To hit a rock on a clear calm night, on a route which had been taken twice a week for seven years, without problem, not surprisingly seems to have produced a total state of shock. Not only was the accident totally unexpected, but happening almost immediately after the change of watches, crew members were still picking up the threads of their responsibilities. The captain's immediate response, on being asked by the mate what had happened, was 'God knows, William'. Meanwhile, Charles Bailey, who had been lying on one of the cabin sofas, ran upstairs to find out what had happened. When he discovered that the ship had hit a rock, he returned to the cabin, to bring Robinson Torry up on deck. On his way to get Mr Torry, he told the passengers in the after cabin that the ship had struck a rock. Some were already in bed. By the time he got Mr Torry to the deck, sailors were already preparing to lower the ship's boats, and passengers were rushing to get on them. No-one was in charge of the filling and lowering of the boats, and the captain complained that he had not given any order for them to be lowered. The orders he did give were for the engine, which Hood, the engineer had stopped at the time of impact, to be restarted, so that the ship could be backed off the rock and turned, with a view to running her ashore on Holy Island. Hood passed the message to Melville, the helmsman, and returned to the engine room to restart the engines.

Confusion reigned on deck. Passengers rushed here and there looking for space in one of the boats. As between the two boats, only some thirty passengers could be accommodated, even in the best of circumstances, this would have been problematic. The port boat was filled, possibly overfilled, and lowered into the water. Both Hildyard and Bailey, seeing the crowd on the port side, decided to get places in the starboard boat. Bailey saw Mr Torry safely placed there, as the boat was beginning to be lowered, and then jumped in after him. They joined a lady already sitting in the bow. Later, Hildyard also dropped into the boat, which was still suspended on the side of the ship. Once there, however, he had second thoughts – he judged the boat to be overcrowded, nor did anyone seem to be in charge. Concluding that he was likely to be safer in the ship, he clambered back up the side, probably making use of mooring ropes or the anchor chain. Two of the ship's firemen, Daniel Campbell, and another unnamed, also tried to save themselves on the starboard boat. There was a further problem – only the boat's bow was free, it was still held to the ship by its stern fastenings, which seemed jammed. At about this time, someone on board shouted, 'Stick by the ship'.

It was now that the captain's order to back the ship off the rock took effect. The ship's great paddles turned, and, in their wash, both ship's boats and all the passengers in them were capsized. According to the time when Charles Bailey's watch stopped in the water, this was at half past midnight. The decision to take the ship off the rock was a total disaster. She was successfully turned and began moving towards the shore, but in the process, she began to fill rapidly with water. Hood again returned to the deck to alert the helmsman to the urgency of getting the ship beached. On his way back, he met William Brown, the mate, only now coming on duty because of the delay in wakening him. One of

Brown's first action seems to have been to order the firing of rockets and a blue light as a signal for help. Back at the engine room, Hood remained by the door, watching his beloved engines being drowned by the water. When nothing more could be done, he returned to the deck, and then climbed the foremast to see if there was any sign of help. There was not.

On deck, it was now a case of every man or woman for themselves – the advice which Captain Miller gave the anxious passengers who surrounded him. It is probable that some of those asleep in the cabins and lounges, never even reached the deck. Those who did dealt in very different ways with the disaster which had befallen them. Some of the crew and passengers attempted to attract attention by shouting together for help. One enterprising soul wrote a message and threw it overboard in a bottle.

> *Pegasus* steamer, to Fern Islands, night of Wednesday, July 19th, 1843. In great distress; struck upon hidden rocks. On board fifty-five persons, vessel must go down, and no Grace Darling.

The bottle was finally picked up off the coast of Holland, early in November 1843[11].

The Reverend Morell Mackenzie, a known strong swimmer, who could possibly have saved himself, instead called the passengers to him, and began to pray. Bailey described how his actions created calm, as passengers knelt round him, joining in the prayers. One lady prayed by herself, as she watched over two young children playing by the companionway, who were oblivious to their danger. Some women clung to the stern of the ship, three took refuge on the ship's masts, as did the ship's carpenter, George Taylor. Hildyard, now back on board, cut some fifteen feet of rope from that lying around, with the thought that he could lash himself to

---

11 *Newcastle Journal* 18 November 1843.

some floating wood when the ship went down. He also removed his hat, boots and stockings, so that he could move more freely through the water. He took up a position at the back of one of the paddle boxes, presumably calculating that he could dive clear of the sinking ship more easily. When the boats had capsized, Bailey had saved himself by grabbing hold of the rudder chain and called to those on deck to haul him up. The mate threw him a rope, and he regained the deck. Then, like Hildyard, he decided to remove his clothes – in his case all of them, before leaping into the sea from the rail of the main rigging.

The captain and the mate had taken up positions on one of the paddle wheel boxes. Although outwardly calm, there is no evidence that in any way the captain attempted to take charge of events. When Hood, the engineer found them, and took his leave of Miller by shaking his hand, the captain's response was 'Good God, we are all going to the bottom'. His last recorded words were 'Great God, look at this'. Hood then made common cause with Thomas Miller, the second mate; together they threw a loose spar of wood overboard and leapt into the water after it, grabbing it for a float.

It was now that the *Pegasus* entered her death throes. She lurched heavily to the port side just before Miller and Hood leapt into the water after their plank, but as the ship righted herself, the men found themselves thrown back on deck. Hood then climbed on to the aftermast, where he clung as the ship now began to sink in earnest, bow first. A few minutes later she again levelled, only this time to sink directly to the bottom. The time was one fifteen a.m. From beginning to end, the sinking of the *Pegasus* took less than an hour.

CHAPTER 13

RECOVERY – DAY 1

Thrown off the mast by the lurching of the sinking ship, the engineer, William Hood, found himself once more in the water. He swam until he was able to catch hold of the gangplank, which was already supporting one of the passengers. Shortly afterwards, Andrew Dowely, the ship's apprentice boy also caught hold of it. The apprentice clung on for some three hours, before exhaustion overtook him, he lost his grip and drowned. The unidentified passenger lasted another hour before also sinking into the water.

The few women, who had clung to the stern of the ship, were now dragged down with its sinking, as were those on the aft and main masts. Part of the foremast remained above water. The carpenter, George Taylor, succeeded in clinging to it despite the violent movements of the ship. After the sinking, he was joined there by Hildyard, who, on surfacing, had grabbed a floating accommodation ladder, sat astride it, and paddled his way to the mast. There the two men lashed the ladder to the mast with Hildyard's rope, which remarkably, he had managed to retain. This gave both men standing room, and they managed to hang on there for the next six hours.

Like Hood, William Brown was thrown into the sea as the ship went down but was drawn underwater by the suction. He surfaced to what he described as a 'fearful scene' – the sea covered with the men and women from the ship, struggling against the waves to keep afloat, shrieks and prayers were heard on every side. He saw the captain swimming – the last record of Alexander Miller alive. Brown managed to grab hold of the engine house hatch. Though it was too small for him to use as a raft, it helped support him in the water. Then nearby, he saw one of the ship's boats, empty of passengers and largely waterlogged, and, using the hatch as a float, he swam to it. Full of water, the boat sat low in the sea. Very carefully lest he capsized it altogether, Brown was able to roll himself into it. He pulled the hatch in after him and laid it across the boat to help steady it. Daniel Campbell, the fireman, found refuge in the other ship's boat.

Charles Bailey was also drawn underwater by the suction of the sinking ship, but, on surfacing, grabbed a piece of wood. He clung to that determinedly, fighting off all other claimants. Louisa Howard, the stewardess, sought his help and tried to grab his hand, but he pushed her away. Similarly, one of the other firemen tried to get hold of the wood, only to have Bailey steer it out of his reach. Nor did he offer any help to young David Scott who floated near him for three hours supported by one of the ship's skylights. What Bailey lacked in humanity, he made up for in narrative power. His account of the wreck, published shortly after his rescue, describes vividly the scene in the water.

> The sky being clear, and the water smooth, I could perceive a great number of persons struggling in the water. Their cries and groans were most awful, and inexpressible. The sound dying away as they sunk, one by one; till all had become silent in death. To me it was like the funeral knell, – the surges dashing sound against those fatal rocks, – and the wild sea fowls screech, hovering over them; as if deeply wailing for the dying and the dead.

About four a.m. he was able to get hold of one of the ship's ladders, which provided better support, but by now he too was becoming exhausted, and wrote that some thirty times the wood slipped from under him, and he had to rouse himself to recapture it.

Despite the rockets fired from the *Pegasus* before she sank, no rescue party came to the aid of the stricken passengers and crew. It was, after all, a calm though not entirely clear night – no watchmen on the land would have been expecting a ship in distress, and as the ship went down towards the back of Holy Island, away from the village settlement, no-one there saw the accident. It was not until after five a.m., some six hours since the *Pegasus* had struck the Goldstone Rock, that the *Martello*, making the return journey from Hull to Leith, under Alexander Blackwood's command, sailed into the wreckage and began searching for survivors.

The first person rescued was William Brown, who though weak, managed to shout loud enough to be heard, and was taken on board. He was then able to tell Blackwood what had happened, and the *Martello* was steered towards the site of the wreck. William Hood was the next to be rescued and was taken to the engineer's room to rest. Then George Taylor and Robert Hildyard were rescued from the half sunken mast. While all this was going on, Charles Bailey's ladder had drifted about a mile and a half from the wreck. With the dawn, a breeze began to blow off the land, and it became ever more difficult to keep hold of the ladder. Nor was he comforted by the attentions of a group of gannets who flew near him, apparently considering the possibilities of a meal. He watched with increasing despair as the *Martello's* boats moved among the wreckage, but never came near where he lay. Finally, after about an hour, one of the boats began to row in his direction, and he was able to attract the crew's attention by waving a stick. He recorded that, as they drew near, they shouted to him, 'Hold on my brave fellow, we will soon have you'. They hauled him into the boat, the second mate taking off his own blue flannel shirt to put on him, and a jacket was wrapped round his legs. So cold was he, however, that when he tried to speak, his teeth bit his tongue. Once on board the *Martello,* he was put to bed and given a glass of hot whisky and water. He slept for about two hours, waking from a nightmare that he was still in the water. Slowly his numbed body thawed out, and with it came both pins and needles from the thawing, and other pains from bruising received in the water.

While the *Martello* was engaged in trying to rescue the living, its strange activities on the water had attracted the attention of fishermen returning to Holy Island from the herring fishing. It was one of those fishermen, George Markwell with his crew, who found Daniel Campbell. What they saw was a man sitting erect in a sunken boat in 'a state of frigid insensibility, with the film of death overspreading his eyes'. Taken on board the fishing boat, he was given some spirits, and began to revive – his first words were about the state of the fires on the *Pegasus*. Markwell then rowed Campbell to the *Martello*, where he was taken on board. Markwell, two other fishermen, Ralph Allison and Alexander Rankine, and the Holy Island harbourmaster, William Wilson, continued to search the wreckage. In all a further six bodies were collected and taken to the *Martello*. Sadly, two, those of a boy, and the second fireman, Alexander Agnew, were still warm, but could not be revived. A young woman was found clutching a small boy in her arms. The bodies of two more women were pulled from the water.

As word of the wreck spread along the coast others began searching. A party of coastguards looking for victims of the wreck set sail from North Berwick at about nine a.m. After sailing south for about fourteen miles, they recovered some floating wreckage, and then the body of a woman. They continued searching until midday when they met with an Aberdeen fishing boat. Discovering that it had already collected several bodies, they transferred their body to that boat. Then, finding that the actual wreck was still further south and that there were many search parties on the water, they returned to North Berwick. What the Aberdeen boat did with the bodies remains unclear, but they may have been included in the count of those taken back to Leith by the *Martello*.

Newspaper reports state that Captain Blackwood spent some seven hours searching the waters in the area of the shipwreck, before resuming his journey north. He finally docked in Leith about seven p.m. on the Thursday, having put into Granton pier some two hours earlier, to land Bailey and Hildyard, as the low tide at Leith would have resulted in a longer delay. Without clothing, property, or funds, however, the two survivors still faced problems. Fortunately, Bailey already knew Charles Gowan, the manager of the *Granton Hotel* tap, and sent a sailor to find him. He came immediately, and organised clothing for them. As Bailey's feet were too swollen for shoes, Gowan took him to his own home which was nearer than the hotel. A doctor was called, medicine administered, and a bed found. The following day, Gowan introduced Bailey to Mr Barry, the hotel owner. He instructed Gowan to get anything else the men needed from the hotel supplies. Later that day, both Barry and Gowan opened subscriptions to raise funds for the men's relief. Bailey recorded that, among others, contributions were made by Messrs Orrell and Wightman, Granton dockyard contractors; Mr Howkins, a local civil engineer; Lord Murray, a guest at the hotel; and Mrs Mackenzie, (wife of John Morell Mackenzie) who probably visited the hotel, seeking news of her husband.

> TO THE EDITOR OF THE SCOTSMAN.
> Granton Hotel, June 22, 1843.
> SIR,—We the undersigned (only surviving passengers from the Pegasus), would feel obliged to you by inserting in your valuable paper, our gratitude for the kind treatment received from Mr Barry, the proprietor of the Granton Hotel, also from Mr and Mrs Gowan of the same establishment, through whose kindness we are very much recovered, and are enabled to proceed on our journey to Hull. In fact, we have received the greatest attention and kindness from all parties, but particularly by the people connected with the Granton Hotel.
>
> CHARLES BAILEY.
> R. HILLARD.

Letter of thanks – The Scotsman 26 July 1843

Once in harbour, presumably the surviving crew members were reunited with their families. The bodies of the dead were moved from the ship to a makeshift mortuary in Leith South Church. Identification could be problematic – unless the body was carrying some kind of named article – letters, inscribed jewellery, even laundry marks, it was difficult to be sure who they were, and in the days before photographs, the only recourse was to publish full accounts of the victims and the clothes they had been last seen wearing. As some of the victims had gone to bed on the ship, even the clothing could not be relied on. Nevertheless, newspapers gave space to detailed descriptions of victims and their clothing, and concerned relatives arranged for handbills to be distributed in the area of the wreck.

At Leith that first day, some were quickly identified – one of the *Martello's* passengers, a Mr Reid, came from Paisley, and was able to identify one of the women as Mrs Christian Alexander, the widow of a Paisley weaver, who had been going to visit her daughter and son-in-law in Hull, and also that the boy was David Scott, the son of a Paisley shawl manufacturer. Maria Barton was identified from a name inside her shoe; the child she had been holding was claimed as James Martin, the son of a London Cabinet Maker, who had also been on the *Pegasus*, but whose body had not yet been recovered.

With the exception of an old lady who was described as being 'partially undressed', all were fairly quickly identified. When no-one had claimed the old lady's body by Saturday, she was interred in the Leith South churchyard. It is possible that Mr Reid's rapid identification of some of the Paisley passengers, allowed those in charge to assume that she had nothing to do with Paisley. The body of Mrs Stewart, the elderly lady from Paisley taking David Scott to London, was never recovered. On 2 September 1843, the *Paisley Advertiser* published a full description of her and an appeal for information about her. Was she possibly the lady who was so hastily interred at Leith? Certainly, there was one identification mistake – the body of the boy identified as James Martin on 20 July, had been returned to the mortuary as 'the wrong body' by 23 July. On its return, the press assumed that it was the body of Field Flowers, the son of the Rector of Tealby, but it was not.

Although accounts are confused, it appears that later on 23 July, it was identified by his father as six-year-old William Elliott, who had been travelling with his uncle James for a holiday in Rochdale.

Before Thursday was over, the news of the sinking was sent to W. Dobson, the secretary of Lloyd's in London, by James Sinclair, their agent in Berwick. The account concentrated on the loss of the ship and was inaccurate in details of the deaths involved, but nevertheless made clear the loss.

> Berwick, July 20
>
> Sir, – I am sorry to have to inform you of the loss of the Pegasus steam-boat, which vessel has been plying between Leith and Hull. It appears that the Pegasus left Leith for Hull yesterday morning, and that she struck upon the Goldstone-rock, near Holy Island, and that she made water, and soon went down. It appears also, that the new Iron steamer Martello, from Hull to Leith, picked up a boat with five passengers in it, and afterwards found 15 bodies floating about, amongst them those of several ladies. A quantity of cargo was also picked up by the steamer.
>
> *The Times* 24 July 1843

A second letter sent the same day from the Leith agent, although still not entirely accurate, did highlight the scale of human lives lost:

> … All hands on board were lost, with the exception of one passenger, three of the crew, and the engineer, who were saved upon pieces of the wreck, and were picked up by the Martello steamer, which arrived here this afternoon, from Hull. About 50 passengers are supposed to have been drowned.
>
> *The Times* 24 July 1843

At the site of the wreck, Captain Blackwood does not appear to have concerned himself with retrieving luggage and other flotsam. For the rest of the day, however, the fishermen searched among the wreckage, both for bodies and items which could be linked to passengers or could have some insurance value. By the end of Thursday, they had found a portmanteau belonging to J. R. Elliott, a box of Mr Elton's stage costumes, addressed to him at the *Theatre Royal*, Richmond, a tin trunk containing what were described as 'Officer's Accoutrements' (specifically cartridge boxes and belts and sabretaches) being consigned to Messrs Raphael and Nathan, Jewellers, Hull,[12] and a carpet bag belonging to the minister, John Morell Mackenzie. Its contents were described in detail and provide an interesting insight into a gentleman's travelling wardrobe – a pocketbook, and loose papers; sponge and bag; morning gown; shirt; hairbrush; comb; shaving tin; toothbrush; tooth powder box; clothes brush; a pair of carpet shoes; silk handkerchief; a pair of cloth boots; a razor case and materials; a pair of leather shoes; and three flannel shirts. In Mackenzie's case, however, there were extras in the shape of books – a Polyglott Bible; Mosheim's *De Rebus Christianorum;* the *Lexicon Biblographicum et Encyclopaedicum* of Mustafa Ben Abdallah Katib Jelabi Vol I; Lardner's Works, Vol. viii (*The Testimonies of Ancient Heathens*); Fabricius' *Bibliotheca Graeca* (an anthology of early Greek writings); and an Ecclesiastical History not now identifiable. Clearly the minister was not a believer in light reading, either in terms of weight or content!

Other items of cargo recovered were a large parcel of sewing silk, a gross of binding sent from William New of Edinburgh to Josiah

---

12 The contents of the tin trunk were much admired by the finders, particularly the sabretaches – pouches used by cavalry officers. These were embroidered in gold and silver wire with the battle honours for Waterloo and The Peninsular Campaign, and the royal monogram for William IV. Presumably they were being sent to the jewellers to have the royal monogram corrected to that of Queen Victoria, but whether they were part of the luggage of one of the soldiers on board, or simply cargo is uncertain. It has been suggested that the regiment most likely to require the refurbishment would have been the 13th Hussars, recently returned from a long period of service in India, but as they were stationed at Canterbury, why would the trunk have been sent south from Edinburgh? *With thanks to Michael Finchen for his help.*

Brunt and Co., Hull, and a parcel of patterns for Goldschmidt and Marcus, Hamburg, from Schwabe and Robert, Glasgow. Alongside these fairly substantial goods, many smaller items were also retrieved, including a basket, a handkerchief marked John Cook, a reticule, and a letter to the captain of the *Pegasus* from Mr Elliott, booking passages on the ship for himself and his nephew. All such items were landed on Holy Island and entrusted to the care of Ralph Gray, coast waiter[13], and the Holy Island schoolmaster, Robert Donaldson.

---

13 Coast waiter was a customs officer who oversaw the landing/shipping of goods coastwise.

CHAPTER 14

RECOVERY – RAISING THE SHIP

By the morning of Friday 21 July 1843, the fate of the *Pegasus* was well known. Initially, the Lloyd's agent, Mr Simpson arrived on Holy Island, along with local reporters from the *Berwick Advertiser* and the *Berwick and Kelso Warder*. Mr Wilson, the harbourmaster, took the group out in his boat to view the site of the wreck – 'nothing is to be seen excepting five feet of her tapering white-painted topmast projecting above the waves, with a yellow ball at the top.' On returning to the Island, the reporters picked over and listed the goods so far salvaged, and had a brief interview with an unnamed employee of the Company, who had been sent to the Island. This was probably William Pringle, John Inkster's deputy. At that time, his best estimate of lives lost was between thirty-six and forty.

Other bodies and goods continued to surface or be washed ashore. Robert Smeddle, the land agent at Bamburgh Castle, became the recipient of bodies taken from the water south of Holy Island. Sadly, it was a task with which he was already familiar. Five years earlier, when the *Forfarshire* sank off the Farne Islands, he had become responsible for organising the inquests on the forty-three passengers and crew who died. It must have been a harrowing experience to find himself once more at the centre of a similar event. That Friday, fishermen from the village of Beadnell, brought him a body of a woman which had been found floating some five miles south of the wreck. He described it in a letter to the Company on the Saturday:

> About five feet six inches high, stout make, dark hair, rather short nose turned up at the point, and supposed to be married

from the ring on her finger; large drop ear rings; had on a muslin de laine dress, open white net stockings, stuff shoes, Tuscan bonnet with black veil, no stays nor pockets on, and no mark upon the linen.

Edinburgh Evening Courant 24 July 1843

Initially Smeddle suggested that the woman might have been one of the soldiers' wives, but eventually, after an affidavit from her father-in-law had been received, she was identified as Mrs Murdoch McLeod from Aberdeen. The body was buried in Bamburgh churchyard on Wednesday, 26 July 1843.

By Saturday, French fishing vessels had joined the search. A chest containing more of Mr Elton's stage costumes was recovered. Relatives of some of the lost were arriving on Holy Island in search of news. Others were arranging for notices to be published and getting in touch with contacts in the area. James Pilley, the Wesleyan Methodist minister at Berwick, was asked by a friend in Perth to try to find the body of David Whimster, and to ensure it had a Christian burial. Whimster, a young man from Edinburgh, had been travelling to Sheffield, to be licensed as a Wesleyan preacher.

While this activity was going on along the Northumberland coast, back in Leith, the Company were making arrangements to raise the *Pegasus*. Robert Cook was placed in charge of recovery operations. They appear to have been confident that the ship could be raised, arranging for an advertisement to that effect to appear in the *Caledonian Mercury* on the Monday:

NOTICE.

MEASURES having been taken to RAISE the Steamer 'PEGASUS,' sunk at the Fern Islands, I have to request that you will inform me as soon as possible, whether (in the event of our succeeding to raise her or save any part of her Cargo), you wish your Goods sent on to Hull or returned to Leith. In either case it is requested that some person be authorised by you to sign the usual [...age] bond, previous to their being forwarded as you may direct.

Supplies of materials and men from Messrs Menzies & Co., with four Lighters and a Steam Tug, have been despatched to-day (22d), to use every exertion in raising the Ship and Cargo to behoof of all concerned.

JOHN INKSTER,

Agent for the Hull and Leith Steam Packet Co. Leith,

44, Bernard Street, 22d July 1843.

On the Saturday, the *Martello* resumed her normal service to Hull. On board were some ninety passengers, including the party of army recruits who had missed the *Pegasus* on the Wednesday, and both Bailey and Hildyard, keen to get back to Hull as soon as possible. She called at Holy Island en route, dropping off Robert Cook, accompanied by William Hood, Daniel Campbell and George Taylor. The crew members had been sent to oversee matters on the ship, once the *Pegasus* was raised. There is a callousness about sending these men back to the scene of their near death so rapidly, which appears shocking today, though less so by Victorian standards. The *Martello* also left two of the lighters which she had towed from Leith to help raise the ship. Later in the day, a second salvage party left Leith. This comprised the steam tug, the *Hero*, towing a raft of logs, the remaining two lighters, and the party of men from Menzies shipbuilders, in the charge of Mr Paton, the foreman carpenter. A youth from Leith seeking information about his father who had been a passenger on the *Pegasus,* persuaded the party to let him sail down with them. Mr Simpson, the Lloyd's agent, continued to monitor the situation of the wreck, writing to London at nine p.m.:

I have just now returned from Holy Island, and beg to enclose you some particulars as to the loss of the ill-fated steamship Pegasus. I have been off to the vessel, and find she is in 10 fathoms of water, 6 fathoms above her rail, and the mast is five feet above the surface at low water.

It does not appear that she has as yet broken up, as the mast is still standing, and very little wreck-wood has driven from her. ...

I understand that an attempt is to be made to weigh the vessel, and preparations are now making for that purpose. ...

The Times 25 July 1843

That evening, the weather worsened as a storm blew in. This diverted men from working on recovery as many more ships sought refuge at Holy Island – twenty-five ships succeeded in taking shelter in the harbour, but five ships needed rescuing. Also, and more seriously from the point of view of the raising of the *Pegasus*, it disturbed the ship and its remaining contents. On Sunday, the trunk containing Murdoch McLeod's clothing was washed up in Waren Bay, opposite the island. On the Monday, a box, possibly the ship's safe, was recovered off North Sunderland. It contained the ship's cargo book and the discharge certificate for Graham Vernon Pegot, a private in the 6th Regiment of Dragoon Guards. The quarterdeck and cabin staircase rose to the surface on Monday evening and were towed to the Island by the fishermen on Tuesday. This led to the recovery of more items:

» a writing desk belonging to William Banks, a young man from Bewdley, apparently returning from a visit to family in Glasgow
» a work box belonging to Sarah Briggs from Hull, returning home after a period of employment as a governess with the Elphinstone family[14]
» a pair of the captain's boots
» a puncheon of whisky, marked Scott & Allan, which was taken by the customs officers
» a number of silver spoons and toddy ladles

---

14 The box had Sarah's name scratched on it, but the fact that the lid bore two capital Es, suggests it may have been a parting gift from the Elphinstones.

»   a silk and fur lined cape
»   a letter and clothing identified as belonging to Fanny Flowers.

The letter appeared in the *Berwick Advertiser* of 29 July 1843:

MY VERY VERY DEAREST FANNY, – I am truly sorry to
have to say good bye to you, but hope it may not be for long. I
wish you a pleasant journey and every happiness during the holidays, for you have little idea of the love I have for you. I hope
I may be able to come and see you to-day. What time do you
start tomorrow? I must stop now, I fear you care little about me,
but I hope I am and ever may remain your sincerely attached.

CHARLOTTE

To Miss Flowers, 43 –   Tuesday, July 13th

During the week further items floated to the surface. On the
Wednesday, a trunk of clothing was recovered from the sea off
Beadnell, by the fisherman, Ralph Dixon. This was identified as
belonging to Isabella Hopton, from the initials embroidered on some
of the clothes. A woman's body (never identified) was washed up
on Newton beach. A box of clothing belonging to George Laidlaw,
from Moniaive, found floating off North Sunderland, was retrieved
by a Musselburgh fisherman, James Miller, on the Friday.

Meanwhile, the salvage operation had been delayed by the weekend storm. The *Hero* and its lighters did not arrive at Holy Island
until six a.m. on the Sunday morning and, as poor weather continued throughout the day, Monday provided the first suitable opportunity for the salvage party to examine the wreck. The *Berwick
Advertiser's* correspondent reported that the party went out that
morning and was still there on the Wednesday when he wrote.
The plans appear to have been to attach chains from the sunk-
en ship to the four lighters, two on each side, and then, as they
pulled away from the wreck, the tightening chains would bring
the ship to the surface. The rival correspondent from the *Berwick
and Kelso Warder*, writing on the Friday, provided more detail.

Various attempts have been made during the present week to weigh the wreck, the parties going back and forward to the wreck every day, ... Yesterday (Thursday) they had got the chains for weighing attached to the sunk vessel, fore and aft, and if the weather continued fair it was expected that they would 'get a weigh at her' with the tide to-night.

Meanwhile, more relatives arrived on Holy Island, and Bamburgh and Belford on the mainland, looking for information. Among them were members of the Elliott family; Sarah Briggs' brother from Hull; and Caroline Edington's husband and half-brother, Alexander Nesbit, from London. The Elliotts, Briggs and Edington all offered £5 rewards for news of their relatives. Mr Edington was also able to identify and claim a satin cloak lined with fur which had belonged to his wife. A friend or relative of William Milne left a description of him with Mr Wilson, the Holy Island harbourmaster.

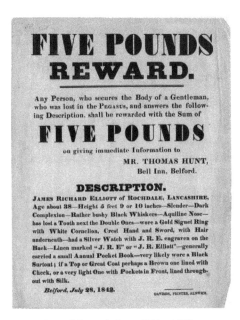

Reward Poster for James Richard Elliott
Northumberland Archives NRO ZMD-167-22-120

By now, growing numbers of sightseers on Holy Island were getting in the way of arrangements for the ship's recovery. Their presence was increased by the crews from some of the ships which had sheltered there after the storm. Particularly unwelcome was the arrival on Thursday of two open carriages of ladies and gentlemen with coachmen in red livery. They were said to be a bathing party from Spittal. They showed little consideration for the nature of the work going on, driving at speed across the sands to the accompaniment of a bugle or French horn. Controlling such interruption was beyond Captain Cook's power, but he did take steps to remove one extra person from the island. The young man who had arrived with the lighters in search of news of his father, and whom the Company had been supporting for the last four days, was now put on a brewer's cart for Berwick, from where he would need to walk the long miles back to Edinburgh.

Although the chains were successfully attached to the *Pegasus* on the Thursday, when the *Martello* had arrived in Hull that afternoon, she reported that the arrangements for lifting the ship were not going well. The exposed position of the wreck left it open to every breeze that blew, from whatever direction. That, together with the ground swell and strong currents, prevented the lighters getting alongside the wreck to begin the lifting process. Consequently, rather than waiting for Saturday's voyage to Leith, as soon as she had discharged her cargo, the *Martello* left Hull for Holy Island, to assist in the raising attempt.

As planned, at high tide on the Friday, an effort was made to raise the *Pegasus*, but while the lighters did succeed in moving her, one of the chains snapped before she could be secured. There had been so many problems in trying to get the various vessels in place for the attempt, that, when the chain broke, it seems to have been decided to abandon the recovery altogether. While accounts speak of the 'chain breaking', it is possible that it could have been the way in which it was secured to the now badly storm damaged wreck that actually gave way. In these circumstances there would have been little chance of a further attempt being successful. Certainly, on Saturday 29 July the *Berwick Advertiser* reported – 'This hope, however, has now vanished ...' The *Hero* and the lighters left for Leith on the Saturday.

Even if the ship could not be raised, attempts had to be made to retrieve the cargo and also the bodies of any persons still trapped within the boat. On the Friday or the Saturday, Lloyd's contracted with John Gann and James Hoult, Whitstable divers, to come up to Holy Island and work on the wreck.

Meanwhile it was important to prevent any other vessel fouling on the wreck remains. On 1 August 1843, Trinity House placed a buoy on the site, and published a notice to that effect in the *Shipping and Mercantile Gazette* of 5 August 1843.

TRINITY-HOUSE. NEWCASTLE, Aug. 1, 1843.
NOTICE TO MARINERS,—A CAN BUOY, painted Green, with the word WRECK in white letters on the head thereof, was this day placed in 9 fathoms water, 40 fathoms dist. N W. from the wreck of the PEGASUS, with the following compass bearings, viz. : —
Goldstone Rock Buoy .... S.S.E. ½ mile dist.
Lighthouses on the Inner Fern Island S.S.E.
Emanuel Head........................... N.W.
Holy Island Castle .... W. by N.
By order,   JOHN CURRIE, Sec.

Newspaper notice to Mariners

Goldstone Buoy today
Photograph courtesy of John Bevan, Holy Island

CHAPTER 15

RECOVERY – THE WORK OF THE DIVERS

When John (Jack) Gann and James Hoult were commissioned to work on the wreck of the *Pegasus,* deep sea diving with the use of a helmet was still in its early years. A Whitstable man, John Deane, had first made use of a helmet into which air was pumped, to combat smoke and to rescue horses from a local stable which had caught fire. With his brother, Charles, he then developed the idea to create a diving suit, so enabling divers to work longer and more freely under water. The first Deanes' diving suit was patented in 1828, and rapidly proved a lucrative invention when used to recover items from sunken ships. James Hoult and the Gann family were among a number of Whitstable fisherman who embraced diving for salvage as a new profession, the Ganns acquiring their first diving suit in 1834.

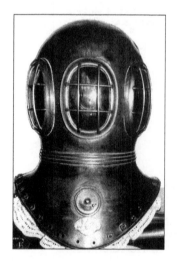

Deane Divers Helmet
Photograph by John Bevan

The suit consisted of a beaten copper helmet with three glasses or port windows, which was supplied with air through a hose connected to a surface supply. The helmet was not attached to the rest of the suit, so that excess air could escape from the helmet into the water.

It was worn with two weights, one on the chest and one on the back. The rest of the suit consisted of a belted tunic and trousers

138

made of Mackintosh's patented waterproof material, and leather shoes. Although the suit allowed the divers to carry out effective salvage work, the great disadvantage was that they had to be careful to keep their heads fairly upright, lest the helmet filled with water.

The divers had arrived at Holy Island and had begun diving on the wreck by Wednesday, 2 August 1843. With their coming, the recovery of bodies, personal possessions and cargo was no longer so dependent on the vagaries of wind and tide, and the newspapers began to report a steady stream of items. The first casualty to be removed from the wreck was the black clad body of George Aird, the son of an Edinburgh grocer, identified by his name engraved on his watch. The watch had stopped at 1.22, giving the time of his drowning. The divers reported that his body had not risen to the surface previously as it had been trapped by timber which had fallen across it. They anticipated that there were more bodies to be found, but that for the present they were buried under mattresses and other debris scattered about the passenger cabin.

Three cases of machinery, part of the ship's cargo were brought up along with a quantity of luggage. Four carpet bags were recovered. Three belonged to passengers – Fanny Flowers, James Elliott, and Arthur Moxham. The last bag bore no name, but was finally identified, from the initials found stitched on the socks inside, as belonging to the captain, Alexander Miller. There were also two trunks, identified as belonging to Mrs Edington and Miss Briggs. Alexander Nesbit, Caroline Edington's half-brother, had remained in Bamburgh, waiting for news of his sister, although Mr Edington, her husband, had returned to Glasgow. Word was sent to Alexander that the trunk had been recovered, and on Thursday morning he wrote to Caroline's sister Jane, to tell her the news:

Bamburgh by Belford August 3

Thursday

My dear Jane

I did not get to Holy Island yesterday in consequence of having made a mistake about the state of the tide and the thickness of the weather. I however have a message from them that a valuable box belonging to our dear Caroline had been brought on shore. It must therefore be the one which contains the Bracelets etc. I however intend starting immediately for that place.

I am sorry to say that I have heard no news of the steamer and the weather is so foggy at sea that even when boats do venture out, they cannot see beyond a few yards around them which is very unfavourable for us ... I spent the day yesterday in absolute idleness my mind weighed down by all sorts of fancies. Today having no object in view I feel more comfortable. I had a famous supper and made an excellent breakfast Eggs & Herring. I have a letter from Edington this morning – it contains nothing new or interesting ...

Extract from letter courtesy of June Slee and Alex Findlater

The divers' work had the additional effect of disturbing the site. On Friday, 4 August 1843, the paddle steamer *Vesta*, sailing from Newcastle to Leith, picked up the body of one of the soldiers, and landed it on Holy Island. The body was described as wearing the fatigue dress of the 96th Regiment, with £3.3s.9d, a tobacco box, knife and keys in the pockets. The face was said to be badly disfigured, and as the body was already decomposing, no attempt was made to search the uniform for an identity. The corpse was buried in the Holy Island graveyard on Monday 7 August 1843.

Further bodies were recovered by the divers on 8 August. The first was a young man, identified from the inscription in the New Testament he was carrying, and a letter addressed to Sergeant Ross, 78th Regiment, as J. McDougall, the new recruit who had been travelling with the Army Recruiting Party. His other possessions were a razor and a small two-bladed penknife. The second body was that of a middle-aged man, identified as a Mr Innes, about whom nothing further is known. At Bamburgh Castle, Robert Smeddle sent out a Bamburgh fisherman, Mr Weatherston, in search of further bodies. He found the body of John Morell MacKenzie floating on the water above the wreck. The body was described as fully dressed, with the exception of the shoes and the hat. The reporter speculated that an unbuttoned waistcoat was a sign that MacKenzie had risen hurriedly from his bed when the ship struck the rock. In the pockets were a purse and two slips of paper, said to contain sermon notes in shorthand. (He had been due to preach in Bedford, where his parents lived, on 30 July). The body was taken back to the Castle, and Smeddle sent word to Edinburgh that it had been found. As a result, one of MacKenzie's friends, William Lindsay Alexander, the minister of the Argyle Square Congregational Chapel, hurried down, with instructions that the body was to be taken back north, to be buried in Edinburgh.

John Morell MacKenzie's gravestone – for the inscription see his entry in the Appendix

When Dr. Alexander arrived at Bamburgh, however, it quickly became clear that the body was too far decayed for this to be a sensible proposition. It was agreed to bury the body at Bamburgh, and Dr. Alexander selected a spot close to the grave of Mr Robb of Dunkeld, one of the victims of the wreck of the *Forfarshire* five years earlier. Mackenzie had himself preached at the Edinburgh funerals of two other victims of the *Forfarshire*, so it seemed an appropriate choice.

While these bodies were being recovered, a salvage sale was also going on. This was for the unclaimed items already brought up by the divers. Prominent among these was the timber of the quarter-deck and the cabin floor. Although no record survives of the sale or the sums made, in the windswept and comparatively treeless area of Holy Island and North Northumberland, it is not difficult to believe that quantities of such fine timber, even soaked with sea water, would have fetched good prices.

On Wednesday, 9 August 1843, the divers retrieved more luggage – Field Flowers' carpet bag, and trunks belonging to Mr Elton, and William Banks. Banks' trunk was said to be a family heirloom. The wood was studded with brass nails, giving the date 1705, and the remains of initials for F.B., an ancestor, Francis Banks. The main diving task over the next few days, however, was to clear the rigging of the ship, and to cut away the remnants of the decks, to allow better access to the holds.

Meanwhile, fishermen recovered more bodies. A Holy Island boat took up a body which was identified as John Brown, a painter from Elgin. He had carried with him letters, the addresses of which enabled the news of his being found to be sent to his brother James in Edinburgh, and his father in Elgin. John himself was buried in the graveyard on Holy Island, alongside a number of the other victims. A Craster fisherman, Joseph Archbold, picked up a woman's body near Boulmer. The body had on a flannel petticoat, stays, and a sleeping gown with the initials IH. It was taken to Craster Tower, where the lord of the manor, Thomas Wood Craster, arranged a coffin for it. From the initials, it was identified as Isabella Hopton, and buried at Bamburgh. A further two bodies, a man and a woman, were found by French fishermen working in the area. The bodies were retrieved, but as they bore no identification and were badly decayed, the fishermen returned them, weighted, to the sea. That day, the divers concentrated on recovering goods. The ship's silver plate was brought up, as was the captain's tin box containing £4.4s.6d., very valuable luggage belonging to Miss Barnetson, and more chests and cargo. Not all the luggage was readily identifiable, and opening the pieces to search for clues could result in tragic finds, as the *Stamford Mercury* reported on 18 August 1843:

> In one box there were many little infant's clothes, all most beautifully made and mended, proving what a careful mother had been with them. Then there were relics of so much affection and so many hopes all destroyed!

That Thursday (10 August), the *Martello*, on her return voyage to Leith, called in to Holy Island, and from there towed a fishing smack laden with some of the recovered goods to Edinburgh.

The reporter for the *Morning Chronicle* wrote that 'the bodies … are found floating in all directions'. It was indeed true. The body of another soldier, never identified, was recovered off Craster, probably on the Friday, though accounts are confused. The same day, at Burnmouth, to the north of Berwick, the herring boat, *Alert*, picked up a badly decomposed body, and brought it into Berwick, the first victim to be landed there. This time the body could be identified. It had on light tweed trousers, a black silk waistcoat and Shetland grey socks. Most importantly the shirt bore a laundry mark 'Wm. Milne. No. 2'. The identification of the body and its landing at Berwick, was critical in enabling an inquest to be held into the cause of the wreck.

Yet more bodies were found over the weekend of 11 and 12 August 1843, again by fishermen. On the Saturday, one of the children lost in the wreck, Field Flowers, was recovered by French fishermen, who gained considerable praise locally for refusing to accept the offered reward of £3, saying that they had 'only performed an act of common humanity'. By a strange co-incidence, Field's uncle, William Henry Flowers arrived on Holy Island, just as the fishermen were bringing Field's body ashore. Field was buried on Holy Island the following day.

Robert Smeddle at Bamburgh Castle took charge of another three bodies, as he described in a letter of 17 August:

> On Saturday last, the North Sunderland fishermen brought me the bodies of a man and a woman – the man about five feet 3 inches high, stout make; had on a brown cloth shooting jacket, with a loose pad underneath, to raise one shoulder to a level with the other, small striped dark cloth waistcoat, with metal sporting buttons, and trousers of the same material; no neck-cloth, and no mark upon linen or stockings. We found in his pockets eight £1 Aberdeen notes, £1.4s. in silver, and one penny, two knives, and a silver pencil, four keys upon a ring, two single keys, and one latch key; and we suppose him to be Mr McLeod from Aberdeen.
> The female was about five feet four inches high, broad across the shoulders; had on a lilac printed cotton gown, white flannel petticoat, marked 'L.H. No. 3.', linen chemise marked 'L.H. No. 1.', calico drawers to cover the body, black worsted stockings, and black cloth boots, had in her pocket a silver watch, a purse containing seventeen shillings and sixpence, a watch guard chain, and a ring on the third finger of the right hand.
> The body of a gentleman was brought to me on Sunday morning last by the revenue cutter, dressed in a brown pilot coat, black dress coat, black satin waistcoat, with a white sprig upon it, black dress trousers, grey socks, and shoes, silver watch, eight pounds in gold, and five shillings in silver, and from the letters found in his pocket, I have no doubt that he is Mr John Colquhoun[15], bleacher, Bridge Street, Paisley, to whose friends I have written, and the body was respectably interred Bambrough churchyard on Sunday last.

---

15 All other accounts give his name as James.

Since writing the above, I have ascertained that the female was Louisa Howard, of Hull, stewardess on board the *Pegasus*; the watch found upon her person has the name of the captain, 'Alexander Miller, Leith, June 1841,' engraved upon it[16].

Berwick & Kelso Warder 19 August 1843

On the Sunday, the Newcastle steamer *Rapid*, reported that the body of a soldier had been seen floating, but no attempt seems to have been made to retrieve it.

At the beginning of the following week, the divers brought up the last bodies from the wreck. On Monday 14 August 1843, they managed to remove one of the firemen, William Knaresborough, from the forehold of the ship. Then, on the Tuesday, a male passenger was recovered. The body was identified as Mungo Easson, a gardener from Dundee. He also was buried on Holy Island. The same day, about a mile out from Berwick, the Spittal fishing boat, *Thomas and Anne*, picked up a body and brought it into Berwick harbour. From there it was taken to the workhouse. There, markings on the stockings, a tattoo on the left arm, and clothing recognised by Mr Pringle, identified it as the captain, Alexander Miller.

The work of the divers seemed to be coming to an end. It was probably the Hull and Leith Shipping Company's intention to make full use of this special resource, which led to the publication of a notice regarding the sale of the *Pegasus* in Newcastle and Berwick papers that week:

---

16 The watch was almost certainly a wedding gift to Alexander, who married his second wife, Margaret Edmond at South Leith church, Edinburgh on 6 June 1841. How Louisa Howard came to be carrying it must remain a matter of speculation.

FOR SALE

THE 'PEGASUS' Steamer, as she now lays sunk at the Farne Islands.

Offers to be received by Mr John Inkster, 44, Bernard Street, Leith. The presence of experienced Divers at the Wreck affords a great facility for Ship carpenters and Engineers in the neighbourhood weighing the Machinery and Boilers at a small expense.

Leith, Aug. 10, 1843

It was now nearly a month since the *Pegasus* had sunk, and the hopes of families and friends that their loved ones would be found must have been fading fast. This sense of despair is evident in the letter Alexander Nesbit, still in Bamburgh, wrote to his half-sister Jane on 16 August:

My dear Jane
I am sorry to say that I have no satisfactory news to offer you but this There is no cause for dispair two more bodies having been found floating yesterday belonging to the ill fated sufferers. I have been much disappointed in not having had the Steamer Boat placed at my disposal yesterday as I expected and as I am completely idle to day I intend going over to Holy Island to ascertain whether there is any likely hood of a desirable arrangement being carried into effect, The Insurers I must say have behaved very indifferently about the business, and have shown a want of feeling really most extraordinary, but which I hope will yet be [visited] on them. The divers were not down to the wreck yesterday on account of a thick fog and I suppose that the same cause will prevent them going down today.
I continue quite well but rather more dull and oppressed since the loss of my fellow sufferers – I take my bathe in the sea as usual and I think derive great benefit from it. I had conceived a kind of hope that I should have a letter from you to day and was silly enough to feel disappointed at its not coming. Write to me my dear sister when you can. Your letters always give me comfort. My imagination being apt to run riot in the absence

of all direct intelligence, the more particularly as I am in any thing but a happy mood at present.

Extract from letter courtesy of June Slee and Alex Findlater

On the Friday, a body was spotted floating off Bamburgh rocks. A boat was launched, and the drowned man brought to shore. Although badly decomposed, he was able to be identified as Thomas Hodgson, the young man from Edinburgh who had been on his way to take up a new job in Leeds with the Mechanics' Institution and Literary Society there. He was buried that evening in St. Aidan's Churchyard in Bamburgh. The next day, a fishing boat found another body on the Goswick Sandridge, a notorious sandbar opposite Holy Island. This proved to be that of James Elliott, the Rochdale lawyer who had been taking his nephew home with him to Rochdale. He was buried on Holy Island the same day. Before the month ended, a foreign fishing boat brought

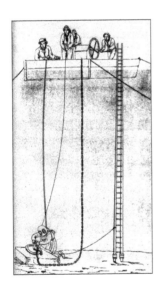

the corpse of Alexander Black into Holy Island. Black, from Dunbar, was an ex-soldier who had been travelling to London in the hope of obtaining a pension from Chelsea Hospital. A Dundee boat recovered the badly decayed remains of William Primrose, removed the identification details and then weighted and sank the body; an unidentified man with a tuft of reddish hair was found off the mouth of the Coquet River, and also re-sunk.

The early divers at work
From Submarine Researches,
Charles Deane, 1836; courtesy of
John & Ann Bevan

On 25 August 1843, having finished their main task, and before returning to Whitstable, Messrs Gann and Hoult put on a diving demonstration for the islanders in Holy Island harbour, showing how they raised property from the seabed. So popular was this, that Robert Wilson, the Spittal pilot, who regularly used his steam tug *Majestic* for sight-seeing trips, laid on a special visit to Holy Island the following Monday, so that visitors from the mainland could see for themselves the work of the divers.

In the following month, several more bodies surfaced. On 20 September, James Martin was recovered and buried on Holy Island. Two soldiers were found – B. Dunn from the 96th Regiment and a W. B. Steward from the 86th. Along with them was a civilian identified as Wetherspoon Connell, whose burial Robert Smeddle arranged at Bamburgh. It was a measure of the extended nature of the process, that by the time these last identifiable bodies from the *Pegasus* were being recovered, the monument to the Reverend J. Morell Mackenzie had been completed and was being erected in Bamburgh churchyard. The final body, that of a boy thought to be between eight and ten years old, and believed to be from the *Pegasus*, was not found until September 1844, when two boys on Holy Island found it trapped among rocks on the shore, seaweed growing on his clothes. Possibly this was the son of one of the soldiers.

In all, the bodies of eight crew, twenty-four civilian passengers and six soldiers were recovered. A further seven unidentified bodies were found. The bodies of five of the crew, ten of the known civilian passengers and possibly nine soldiers and family members were never recovered. As there was no formal record of the steerage passengers, it is impossible to say how many of them were lost, but on the basis of the those recovered and those known of but never found, approximately seventy people must have drowned when the *Pegasus* went down.

CHAPTER 16

INQUIRY

Why the *Pegasus* should sink on a calm and relatively clear night, whilst on a passage which she had sailed weekly for over seven years, was a matter of great interest and much speculation. From immediately after the wreck of the *Pegasus*, the pressing question was *How could it have happened?* It was a question which not surprisingly the relatives wanted answered. It was a question posed regularly in the editorials and letter pages of the newspapers. It was a question which a considerable number of armchair pundits pontificated upon, often with little regard for truth or accuracy. There were a number of close to libellous statements that the Company ran their business solely for profit, with no regard for the safety of passengers, completely disregarding the major refit undergone by the *Pegasus* eighteen months before. She was described as worn out; it was alleged that she was probably racing, although there was no evidence of other ships in the vicinity. There was a clear need to get at the actual facts and make them known.

From the time of the sinking, what everyone had agreed on was the need for some competent investigation. On 29 July 1843, the *Newcastle Journal* had asked for a Public Inquiry. The *Berwick Advertiser* followed this up on 5 August in terms which have quite a modern ring:

> The Government, we think, could do well to authorise a commission to inquire into the whole circumstances of the case. In hundreds of instances the public money is squandered on far less important objects.

Sometime before 9 August 1843, W. Dobson, Secretary at Lloyd's, wrote to James Edington, the husband of the victim, Caroline Edington:

> With an expression of deep condolence at the bereavement you have sustained, permit me to state that I feel convinced the most searching inquiry must and will be made into this most distressing case by the proper authorities, with the view to prevent a similar calamity in future, and as some satisfaction to the afflicted relatives and friends of those who have lost their lives on this occasion.[17]

As it happened, a mechanism for such an enquiry was already in existence. On 16 February 1843, the House of Commons had set up a Select Committee *'to inquire into the Shipwreck of British Vessels; and the Means of Preserving the Lives and Property of Shipwrecked Persons'*. By the time of the sinking of the *Pegasus*, the committee had nearly completed their report, which had concentrated on the loss of sailing ships. The loss of two steamships, the Royal Mail Steam Packet Ship *Columbia*, off Nova Scotia at the beginning of July, and that of the *Pegasus*, however, resulted in the committee determining to produce a second report, looking more closely at steamship issues. On 27 July 1843, Sir Howard Douglas, M.P., on behalf of the committee, wrote to the Company requesting the names of such of the survivors 'as the Company deem most competent to give evidence before the Committee of the House of Commons on Shipwrecks'. The letter ended up on Thomas Barclay's desk, and he replied on 29 July:

> ... Most unfortunately there are only six survivors – 4 of the crew & 2 passengers – the 4 of the crew are well behaved men in their various situations and you will probably summon them

---

17 The 1843 Lloyd's Letterbook is lost, but this letter was quoted in the *Witness (Edinburgh)* of 9 August 1843.

all if you do not think the engineer's evidence may render the fireman's unnecessary – the two passengers as all that are saved you will want to see both – where there are so few it might be as well to examine the whole six.

Their names are:

1) Wm. Hood First Engineer and 2) Daniel Campbell, Fireman – these two are now at the Fern Islands, part of a force endeavouring to lift the vessel – as that has to be abandoned they will be found at Leith in a few days – if not left, their address is 'Care of Capt. Cook, Pegasus, Holy Island, Belford'.
3) Wm. Brown, First Mate – he is about to sail from Glasgow to Leith round the north in the Co's steamer Glenalbyn – will be in Leith on Saturday next.
4) George Taylor, Carpenter – if not at the Fern Islands he will be at Leith.
5) Hallyard, son of a clergyman in Yorkshire, and 6) Baillie of Hull, a porter, in charge of an infirm gentleman – I do not know more of their addresses – both went to Hull per Martello Steamer – they will be heard of at Hull.

If there be any other information we can furnish you with as to this most distressing event, or assistance in your enquiries we shall be most anxious to give it to you.

University of Glasgow Library, Archives & Special Collections UGD 255/4/17/5/4

As a result of these letters, on 8 August, 1843, after the evidence of the captain of the ill-fated *Columbia,* Robert Hildyard, William Brown and William Hood appeared before nine members of the Select Committee. In many respects the information they offered simply reprised that already given to the press. Robert Hildyard, the only surviving passenger interviewed, was the first to give evidence. The Select Committee began by establishing that he was an experienced merchant seaman, having been sailing across the globe for upwards of ten years, although, as they later discovered, he had not served in steamships. In describing what happened when the *Pegasus* struck the Goldstone Rock, he gave a detail which had not previously emerged in accounts of the wreck – that after hitting the rock, the ship itself recoiled, and it was this which resulted in the sudden inrush of water. He thought that the restarting of the engine had been an attempt to get the damaged ship to the shore.

Hildyard was pushed to give his opinion of the captain's actions in these last critical minutes. Although forced to concede that it might have been better if the ship had remained wedged on the rock, he gave as his final opinion that 'I think he did everything in his power for the preservation of the ship'. Questioning now moved on to the ship's boats. Hildyard confirmed that there were two ship's boats and judged that each was capable of holding some eighteen people, but he thought that there were about fifty-four people on board. The confusion which surrounded the lowering of the boats was then described. Hildyard explained that he had first got into the starboard boat, but seeing no-one in the boat who appeared to know anything about sailing such boats, he got out again. He accounted for his survival by saying that when he got back on board, he cut two fathoms of rope from a triple braid coil. He fastened the ends together and put the rope round his neck, intending to use it to lash himself to some floating wood. Not seeing any, he tried unsuccessfully to rip off the engine room door, but in the end, he was able to use the rope to lash himself to the mast. The select committee now turned its attention to the sobriety of the captain and the crew. Initially, Hildyard said that he thought the Captain was 'pretty sober', an answer too vague to satisfy the committee. Finally, on being re-questioned, he stated that the captain was 'perfectly sober', and that he had not seen him drink anything.

William Brown, the first mate, was the next witness. Initially, he was questioned about the position of the Farne Islands navigation lights at the time of the accident, and stated that, when he came on deck, they were not in the correct alignment. He suggested that the problem may have been the result of confusion caused by fishing boat lights. Like Hildyard, he stated clearly that the *Pegasus* had rebounded from the rock and was quite sceptical that the ship could have been kept on the rock. He confirmed Hildyard's estimate of the shortfall in places on the ship's boats, and agreed with the committee's questioning that if the ship had had paddle-box boats[18] it was likely that everyone could have been saved. When asked about the confusion over the lowering of the boats, he confirmed that neither he, nor the captain, had given the orders:

> We had no idea she would fill so fast. We thought to have got her
> on the land, but the water rushed in so fast it put out the fires.
> Select Committee Report

Questioning now moved to the wisdom of taking the inside passage. Provided the weather was good, as it had been that night, Brown stated that he would have had no hesitation in taking the same route – it made for a shorter journey and one which could be done more quickly, saving at least half an hour. Under further questioning, however, he conceded that, going forward, he would never again take the inner passage at night. He agreed with committee members, that if there had been lights either on Holy Island or on the Goldstone Rock, the accident would have been avoided, and that watertight bulkheads might also have prevented the sinking. The select committee's last questions to him focused on the sobriety of the captain and how he himself had been saved. His account of being saved added nothing to what was already in the public domain. Regarding the captain, he agreed with the questioner that the captain was generally a sober man; when pushed, he added that he had only once seen

---

18 Paddle-box boats were boats made to fit the paddle-box rim, stowed bottom upwards on each box.

him the worse for liquor at sea, and that even then, he was perfectly capable of taking charge of the ship.

The final witness was William Hood, the ship's engineer. The questioning followed a similar format. The select committee established that, after striking, the inrush of water had extinguished the boiler fire in about fifteen minutes. Again, they asked about paddle-box boats, and were again told they might have saved everyone; again, they asked about the captain's sobriety, and were told 'I think he was sober'. Like Brown, Hood offered no criticism of taking the inner passage, provided the lights were visible. Hood also agreed that, if there had been a light on Holy Island, the ship might not have struck the Goldstone, and that a water-tight bulkhead in front of the engine, could have enabled the fires to be kept burning until the ship was run aground on the shore.

In keeping with their remit, the main concern of the select committee had been to identify ways in which more lives could be saved in future accidents. All three witnesses were the subject of much leading questioning in relation to paddle-box boats, and water-tight bulkheads. Although interested in the causes of the wreck, the committee did not concern itself with attributing blame. Therefore, it was not surprising that when their second report was published on 15 August 1843, as well as several recommendations relating to ships in foreign waters, the recommendations which related to the *Pegasus* were '*the importance of all sea-going Steamers being fitted with Paddle-box Boats, irrespective of Life-Boats and other Boats; and that such Steamers should be built with water-tight divisions*'.

The committee's recommendations, although significant for the future safety of shipping, did not meet the strongly felt need of the friends and relatives of those lost in the *Pegasus*, and of the local communities where she sank, to establish exactly why the wreck had taken place and who or what was to blame. The hope was that this could be achieved through a coroner's inquest on a body or bodies from the wreck. With so many bodies recovered within days of the sinking, this should not have presented any difficulty, but it did. The first bodies, picked up by the *Martello* on the morning of the accident, were taken straight to Leith, thus removing them from the jurisdiction of an English coroner. The opportunity lost. The first attempt to convene an inquest occurred when a woman's body was recovered near Beadnell, in Northumberland, on 21 July 1843. When an application was made to the Northumberland coroner, it was to discover that both the coroner at Alnwick, Mr Russell, and the Newcastle coroner, Mr Reid, were in London. As the body was already decomposing, a magistrate's order was obtained to bury it immediately. A second opportunity had been lost. Then the divers brought up the body of George Aird from the sunken ship and landed him at Holy Island.

Administratively, Holy Island, for reasons of history, was part of North Durham, a detached portion of Durham county, not of Northumberland. This anomaly was in the process of being resolved by Act of Parliament in the summer of 1843. So, when the vicar on Holy Island wrote to the Durham coroner, asking him to hold the inquest, he replied, saying that under legislation passed in the current session of Parliament, he was prevented from holding inquests in North Durham, and the Alnwick coroner should be asked to conduct it. Unfortunately, the Alnwick coroner was still in London, so the body was buried without an inquest. A third opportunity had been lost. It was not until Friday, 11 August 1843, after the evidence had been given to the select committee, and fully three weeks after the sinking, that a way was found out of the vicious circle. On that date, the body of William Milne was landed at Berwick-upon-Tweed. Berwick was its own jurisdiction and had its own coroner – at long last an inquest could be held. The body was taken to Berwick workhouse, and a jury of local tradesmen[19] was empanelled. Even then, in charge was an acting coroner, R. B. Weatherhead, as the official coroner, Benjamin Nicholson, was suffering from a severe illness.

The inquest opened with one of the Eyemouth fishermen, Thomas Cormack of the *Alert*, giving evidence about the finding of the body. Returning home after fishing at North Sunderland, the crew had seen the body floating in the water about a mile north of Emmanuel Head. This was followed by the workhouse medical officer, Andrew Henderson, giving evidence on the cause of death, which he stated to be *suffocation by drowning*. So far so good, but it was now necessary to show that this dead body had come from the *Pegasus*. The Lloyd's agent, James Sinclair, was called, but declined to give evidence regarding Milne's presence on board, since a member of the Steam Packet Company, Mr Pringle, was on the island and was in a position to provide this information. A letter was sent to Pringle, requesting his attendance, and the inquest was adjourned until Monday. Letters were also sent to the relatives of Miss Briggs and Mrs Edington who were staying in the area, asking if they wished to be present. All declined but indicated how important they felt an effective inquiry was. On Monday, 14 August 1843, the inquest reconvened at the Guildhall, but there was no Mr Pringle. The meeting was adjourned for a further day, but now a summons was issued for Pringle's attendance.

When Tuesday came, William Pringle put in an appearance, claiming that his failure to appear the previous day was due to

---

19 Details of the jury and a full account of the inquest can be found in the *Berwick and Kelso Warder* of 26 August 1843. The jurors were: James Jaffrey, stationer, foreman; George Young, grocer; Grindley Weir, leather cutter; Thomas Thompson, draper; George Weatherhead, confectioner; George Smith, draper; John Davidson, druggist; Walter Kirkwood, draper; James Smail, draper; Alexander Melrose, shoemaker; Alexander Meikle shoemaker.

the message not having reached him. Even now there was more delay. Pringle's passenger list was still on Holy Island, and he would not answer for Milne's presence on the ship without it. The inquest was then adjourned until Friday 18 August 1843 at six p.m., and Pringle was bound over to attend. Before the jury departed, news came that another body had been recovered, and it was agreed to extend the remit of the inquest to both bodies. The new body was thought to be Alexander Miller, but an unambiguous identification was necessary. The coroner and the jury moved to the workhouse where the decaying corpse lay. As we have seen, this was then identified as Captain Alexander Miller.

The inquest resumed as planned on the Friday evening, continued into Saturday and concluded on the following Monday morning, 21 August 1843. As well as providing the list of the booked first-class passengers, Pringle explained that the reason there was not such a list for the steerage passengers, was that their fares were collected by the mate after the ship had sailed. The accounts of the inquest also include the information that, according to Pringle, the *Pegasus* was not insured. The Company's records, held at Glasgow University Archives, however, show the renewal of the *Pegasus'* annual insurance for the sum of £1,000 with the North British Insurance Company on 26 December 1842. This discrepancy does rather call into question the appropriateness of Pringle acting as spokesman for the Company, especially, since as far as is known, Captain Cook, one of the Company's partners, was still on Holy Island.

Pringle himself made clear in his evidence that he was not, in any true sense, the Company's agent – merely their cashier. His information on the history of the ship tended to be vague, and it was only when the deputy coroner focused on the departure of the *Pegasus* on her final voyage that his evidence became more detailed. He had been at the quay that afternoon to give the captain the list of the booked passengers, and then became involved in the dispute with the drunken soldiers. He also gave evidence on the state of the captain at the time of sailing.

Deputy Coroner: Can you say what state Captain Miller was in before sailing? Was he perfectly sober?

Pringle: I should say so; he took his station on the bridge as steady as ever I saw a man go out of the port of Leith.

Deputy Coroner: Were you sensible of any smell of liquor upon him?

Pringle: I did not go upon the bridge, but when talking to him in the cabin, I did not even feel the flavour of liquor.

Deputy Coroner: Was he sober, sir?

Pringle: To the best of my knowledge and belief, upon my oath.

In addition to Pringle, crew members William Hood, Daniel Campbell and William Brown were examined on the events of 19 and 20 July, and then evidence was sought from local captains as to appropriate routes along this section of the coast. Once it had been formally established that Milne was a passenger on the *Pegasus* and the actual events surrounding the sinking were described, the questioning moved on to broader issues:

»   the seaworthiness of the ship
»   the competence and sobriety of the captain and helmsman
»   the speed of the ship
»   attempts to summon help
»   the route of the ship.

Hood, Campbell and Brown all described the events of the night as they had experienced them. Again, these did not add much to what was already in the public domain. Hood and Campbell, however, stated that the captain complained that the lifeboats had been lowered by the passengers without his orders. All the men asserted that the ship was in good seaworthy condition and had undergone a major refit eighteen months earlier. They were also clear that the captain had commanded their respect, was strict and sober, and although less was said about Robert Melville, the helmsman, he also was believed to be sober and reliable.

A considerable amount of questioning focused on the speed of the ship. The press had contained some allegations that the ship was speeding, in an effort to show that she could go as fast as the new *Martello*. This was denied and the crew members were in general agreement that on the night in question she could not have been travelling at more than seven or eight knots, although, in the right conditions, she could make ten knots. There was, however, a problem. Hood said he had checked his watch at the Bass Rock when it showed eight-thirty p.m. If the *Pegasus* was only doing seven or eight knots, she could not have reached the Goldstone by twelve-thirty a.m. Similarly, Brown gave evidence that the ship had reached Fast Castle three hours after leaving Leith, a speed of twelve knots. This resulted in more detailed questioning of the witnesses, without any definite outcome, although both men suggested that they might have made a mistake in the times they stated. What did emerge was that the use of both engine and sail together could create some uncertainty as to the exact speed of the ship.

Hood stated that a blue light and two skyrockets were fired to summon help, but not the ship's quarter pounder swivel gun. Campbell had seen the blue light but not the rockets. He added that the crew and passengers agreed to raise a shout together. The mate, Brown, confirmed that he had fired both light and rockets. None were confident that the blue light, usually a signal that a passenger needed to disembark, was a recognised emergency signal. Later, Ralph Mossman, master of the Berwick Shipping Company's steamer, *Rapid*, gave evidence that the blue light was a recognised distress signal.

The most detailed questioning focused on the ship's route and why she had hit the Goldstone on a clear, calm night. The normal route taken by the *Pegasus* was described – she sailed to the west of the Goldstone, closer to Holy Island, but then turned towards the Megstone, passing east of it; and sailing between it and the Big Farne, before continuing south. Much of this evidence was highly technical and related to the alignment of various navigation lights. This route, it was said, lessened the effect of the tide, the force of which was broken by the Big Farne. It was also established, as in the evidence to the parliamentary select committee, that the closer the ship steered to the Goldstone, the shorter the passage was. Now, William Brown altered the evidence he had given to the select committee. In response to a question as to whether he considered the route safe at night, he replied: '*No, I never approved of the passage at night. In day time it is safe enough*'.

Both Mossman and David McDonald of the General Shipping Company's schooner, *Adelaide*, also stated that they considered the Goldstone passage dangerous. Even so, explanations of why a route usually navigated safely, had gone so wrong early in the morning of 20 July, were very limited. Brown thought that they had steered to avoid some fishing nets off Berwick, and this must have put them out of the correct alignment. The other captains, however, were very clear that between the coastline and the visible lights, it was relatively easy to establish exactly where a ship was. The overall conclusion was that the watch, for whatever reason, was inadequate. Given that the two men on the bridge were the captain and his brother, and that the brother failed to waken the mate at midnight as was customary, was it possible that the two men were engaged in some family discussion or argument which distracted them from the task in hand? As neither survived, it must remain a mystery.

At about one o'clock on the Monday afternoon, after an hour's consideration, the jury gave its verdict.

That the persons on whose bodies they had held inquest had met with
an accidental death, occasioned by the gross negligence of the captain
and those on the look-out of the vessel on board of which they were.

As well as this damning verdict, they also applied the old medi-
aeval punishment of levying a deodand (that is, where something
was the immediate cause of the death of a human being, it, or
part of it, was forfeited to the crown to be applied to pious uses)
on the ship of £100 for each case – £200 for the two bodies
on which the inquest had been held. They added that the vessel
was so badly equipped that they had no sufficient means to make
signals to the shore. Finally, they made one recommendation:

That all steam vessels ought to have sufficient boat accommodation to
carry the whole of the passengers on board.

Even now, the saga of the inquest was not over. The HLSPC appealed against the verdict, largely on technicalities. Application
was made in the Bail Court, early in November 1843 for the verdict to be quashed. Grounds included that:

» The record did not show that the inquest had been held upon
   a view by the jury of the body of the deceased.
» The Berwick coroner was not empowered to award any deodand.
» It was not the ship per se that was the cause of death, but the
   carelessness of the crew.
» The verdict did not refer to the date of the victims' death.
» The victim (Milne) may not have been on board at the time
   of the death.
» The Company was misdescribed as the *Hull and Leith Shipping*
   Company, whereas it was the *Hull and Leith Steam Packet*
   Company.

Mr Justice Patterson accepted the application and quashed the
verdict.

A question which was never pursued at either enquiry was about the impact of the change of watch so close to the time of the accident – if the ship was off route, there was little or no time for the new watch to identify the problem and adjust the steering accordingly. Interestingly, although it was never given formally as a reason, Charles Bailey, who, of course was not a witness in either investigation, had no hesitation in attributing the accident to that particular event in his published account of the wreck.

> ... I unhesitatingly declare that, I believe the sole cause of the loss of the Pegasus, to have been occasioned by the changing of the watch, between Emanuel Head and the Goldstone rock.

As for the recommendations which were made, it took the sinking of the *Titanic* in 1912, to ensure that all ships had adequate life-saving equipment for all passengers; and it was rules, introduced by Lloyd's Register in 1855, which resulted in shipbuilders introducing watertight bulkheads, to be certain of obtaining insurance.

CHAPTER 17

AID FOR THE VICTIMS

When the *Martello* brought Hildyard and Bailey, the surviving passengers from the wreck into Leith, it was Mr Barry of the *Granton Hotel* who took them in. Not only did he feed and clothe them, but he also launched an appeal on their behalf. Some accounts suggest that this appeal was then extended to support families of other victims, often in dire straits having lost their breadwinner so unexpectedly, but this is not clear. There is no doubt, however, that a fund to help the relatives was launched. A number of fundraising events were held for it, including two pleasure sails. On 11 September 1843, the London, Leith, Edinburgh and Glasgow Shipping Company's ship, the *Royal Adelaide*, made a pleasure trip from Granton to the Bass Rock, the Isle of May and Queensferry, in aid of the families of the *Pegasus*' crew. Tickets were three shillings for the cabin and two shillings steerage, with food available – one shilling for lunch, six pence for a sandwich. Sadly, there is no record of how much was raised, but the company was not entirely altruistic. The *Royal Adelaide* was returning to service after substantial repairs, so the publicity would not go amiss. On 16 September 1843, Robert Cook sailed the *Martello* on a pleasure trip from Hull to Bridlington with all profits to the appeal. As the report of this states that twenty shillings was raised, it may be that a trip in one of the ill-fated Company's vessels was not entirely popular.

The distribution of the funds raised became the responsibility of *The Committee for Granting Relief to the Relatives of the Unfortunate Sufferers in the Pegasus Steam Ship*. Records of the Committee do not seem to have survived, but two appeals to them for help remain in the archives of the Company at Glasgow University. Both relate to the relatives of William Primrose, the stonemason. The first, on 13 September 1843, came from John Laughland, the brother of Primrose's wife, stating that his sister 'is within a week of her Accousement (sic), if you could give her anything per Account to help her in the meantime, it would be thankfully received by her in her present circumstances'. He enclosed with it a copy of the couple's marriage lines, as a proof that she was a genuine claimant. A second letter came from a Thomas Morton of Kilmarnock. He wrote:

> This is to Certiface (sic) that William Primrose, a tenant of mine for many years in Kilmarnock, now at 67 Centre Street Glasgow & also his son William, who was unfortunately lost in the Pegasus Steamer. This man was a great support to his parents & they were at Great pains in Educating him for his Business & as he had a particular Taste for Drawing, they spent a good deal of money on him in that department when they could very ill afford it, & by this unhappy event all their bright prospects are gone forever from him, and his parents being in poor Circumstances on account of his father having nearly lost his eye sight that he is unable to earn anything for the support of his family, & as I understand there is a Committee for assisting the Relatives of those who were lost in that ill fated vessel, the Committee could not give to more needful and deserving people than William Primrose who has been nearly blind this nine years past, As knowing them well, I most Humbly Recommend them the Notice of the Committee, & what makes the case worse is the young man was only married a few days before the Catastrophe Happened, & I am sure which ever aid will be given will be thankfully Received.[20]
>
> University of Glasgow Library, Archives & Special Collections UGD 255/4/17/5/5

---

20 Spelling and punctuation partially modernised to assist understanding.

Even the fairly hard-bitten businessman, Thomas Barclay, must have been touched by their plight, writing to the Leith Office in March 1844, that, as there were few claimants, the Company should try to get as much as possible for the Primroses, who had visited the Company's offices on several occasions. He added that, personally he had given the family twenty shillings and forty shillings shortly after the accident and had called on them.

Another appeal for help, perhaps wrongly directed, was less successful. This was a petition on behalf of the widow and infant child of James Martin, carpenter and upholsterer of 8, Russell Street, Covent Garden, sent by David Smith of the London County Fire Office to Lord Breadalbane.

> … Mr Martin had recently commenced business – and having expended all he possessed in the great consequent outlay, went to Scotland accompanied by his son (a fine intelligent boy 10 years of age) for the purpose of raising the funds necessary to enable him to pursue with success the business he had entered on. – He was on his return in the highest spirits – having a considerable sum of money in his possession – when the unfortunate vessel was wrecked and he and his boy sank to rise no more.

> The widow is thus plunged into the deepest distress both mental and pecuniary (the money lost being required for rent due last midsummer) & I have ventured to address your Lordship in the hope that in addition to the many instances of your kind hearted benevolence you will allow me to place your name amongst those who are striving to alleviate her sufferings by raising a sum sufficient to free her from present embarrassments and enable her to carry on the business for the support of her and infant child.'
>
> National Records of Scotland GD112/11/10/8A/26

Breadalbane, however, instructed that a reply be sent stating that there were already so many claims upon him from his estates and Scotland generally that he could not help. Perhaps if Smith had explained that Martin had moved to London from Edinburgh, he might have been more successful. Some of Martin's other friends, however, must have helped, as his widow, Mary, continued to live at 8 Russell Street at least until June 1845.

The plight of one particular family attracted much attention, that of the actor, William Elton. He left behind seven orphan children, whose ages ranged from Esther, the eldest at twenty-four, to Lucy Emma, the youngest surviving, aged eight. The divers working on the wreck of the *Pegasus*, generously made over to his children their 40% share of the salvage of Elton's possessions, as did the Holy Island pilot. The theatre world was also quick to act on the children's behalf. On Saturday, 22 July, Mr Murray, the manager of Edinburgh's *Adelphi Theatre*, where Elton had been performing prior to sailing south on the *Pegasus,* announced a benefit performance at the theatre on 5 August 1843 for the children, as reported in the *Caledonian Mercury* of 22 July 1843:

SATURDAY EVENING, August the 5th,
Has been appointed for the
BENEFIT OF THE CHILDREN
OF THE
LATE MR ELTON,
On which occasion the Patronage of the Citizens of Edinburgh
is most earnestly and respectfully solicited.
Any Donation from those who may be unable to attend on the
above occasion will be received, and thankfully acknowledged,
by the Public's obedient servant, W. H. MURRAY.

This announcement immediately brought in numerous donations well before the performance, including £5.0s.0d. from the proprietor of the Glasgow *Theatre Royal*, together with arrangements for a second benefit to take place in Glasgow. These plans resulted in an immediate letter of thanks from a friend of the Elton family, Mr McIan:

If you could but see the bereaved family, as I have just seen them, you would indeed feel the full necessity of what Edinburgh is so generously doing. In the name of his seven orphans (you will imagine how incompetent they are now to do it themselves), I thank all who have so liberally come forward; and may they never know the sorrow our beloved friend's fate has brought upon us and his poor children.

Quoted in The Scotsman 28 July 1843

The Edinburgh benefit raised 'upwards of £200'. The idea was taken up by other theatres where Elton had performed, and on 26 July 1843, the rising author, Charles Dickens, gave his support to such fundraising by planning benefit performances at the *Haymarket* theatre:

THE ORPHAN FAMILY of the late Mr W. Elton – A Committee is formed for the purpose of arranging a BENEFIT for the seven fatherless and motherless CHILDREN of Mr W. ELTON, late of the Theatre Royal, Drury-lane, a sufferer to the fatal wreck of the Pegasus. The performances will be announced as soon as possible; in the meantime offers of professional service on the occasion will be gratefully received, as well as subscriptions in money, by

CHARLES DICKENS, Chairman.
The Times 26 July 1843

The benefit raised £280 and was notable for a poetic epitaph on the actor, written by Thomas Hood, which contrasted the sufferings of the actor playing his role in a tragedy, and the reality which had befallen him. Its final lines linked the loss of their father to the fate of the orphans:-

He who could move the passions – moved [by] none,
Drifts, an unconscious corse! – poor Elton's race is run.
Sigh for the dead? Yet not alone for him!
O'er whom the cormorant and gannet swim!

Weep for the dead! yet do not merely weep
For him who slumbers in the oozy deep!
But, like Grace Darling in her little boat,
Stretch forth a saving hand to those that float.
The Orphans Seven! So prematurely hurl'd
Amidst the surges of this stormy world;
And struggling – save your pity, take their part –
With breakers huge enough to break the heart![21]

Theatrical benefits also took place at the *Surrey* (£180); the *City of London* (£50); the *Princess's Theatre*; the *Amphitheatre*; *Sadlers Wells*; the *Victoria*; *Astley's*; and the *Theatre Royal, Brighton*.

Charles Dickens does not seem to have been a close friend of Elton, but the two men had known each other through Elton's work as Chairman of the General Theatrical Fund – a charity for actors suffering hardship. Probably spurred on by his own memories of an unhappy youth, Dickens did not limit himself to promoting fundraising events. Almost as soon as the news of the wreck reached London, he appealed to his good friend, the wealthy philanthropist, Angela Burdett-Coutts to assist him with practical help for the family.

> If in the great extent of your charities, you have a niche left to fill up, I believe in my heart this is as sad a case as could possibly be put into it. If you have not, I know you will not mind saying so to me.
>
> Letter 26 July 1843

Then, on 7 August 1843 he launched a second more general fund-raising appeal on behalf of the children. This was opened by a donation of £30 from Queen Victoria, and through a series of

---

21 The full text quoted in the Domestic Journal and Home Miscellany of Instruction and Amusement Vol. 1, 1849.

letters, Dickens secured both financial and practical support for the Elton Fund. Dickens himself, the M.P. Thomas Talfourd and the banker Edward Marjoribanks became its trustees. In December 1843, a final figure for the appeal was announced – it amounted to the not inconsiderable sum of £2,380.

Meanwhile, the immediate hardship of the family was alleviated by Angela Burdett-Coutts who provided Dickens with money to provide for their needs, some accounts say for the next six months, and Dickens took seriously the task of disbursing it:

> Finding it exceedingly difficult in the midst of their trouble to arrive with anything like tolerable certainty at the weekly expenses of the family; last Thursday, I placed £10 – the ten you sent me – in the hands of a lady who knows them, and can be trusted to make a careful report: and begged her to account to me for it, and to get me an estimate by the time we meet again (next Monday) of their average bills.
>
> Letter to Angela Burdett-Coutts 7 August 1843

The following week, he had ascertained the weekly expenses to be £3. He was astute enough to recognise the risk that so-called friends of the family and others, might seek to take advantage of the children. A particularly nasty example of this emerged in October 1843 when a bottle found washed up on the Norfolk coast, was said to contain a message from Elton – 'Pegasus – God help us – she's sinking. the bottle's empty, 'twill swim, and we also into eternity. Farewell – Elton'.

Dickens was able to obtain the message, which proved to be a forgery, and he was left raging at the cruel hoax – if he had his way, he wrote, he would have the perpetrator flogged at the church door.

Dickens met with the eldest daughter Esther, to discuss the way forward for the family. He, Miss Burdett-Coutts and the *Elton*

Fund Committee then involved themselves in ways of enabling the young people to become self-sufficient. After discussion, it was agreed that Esther should train as a teacher at the National School Training College at Whitelands House – a training course, which was successfully completed in the autumn of 1845, after which she went on to take charge of a school in Mitcham. In January 1844, the committee advertised for one of the Elton girls to take up a position as a companion, but it is not clear which girl, or whether such a post was found. In May 1844, the committee paid for the second daughter, Rosa, to accompany a friend of her father to Nova Scotia where she was able to earn a living giving music lessons, before returning to England in 1846. Later, in 1847, they provided her with a £10 dowry on her marriage. The third daughter, Rosalind, learned wood engraving at the London *Female School of Design*. Unspecified support was also offered to the only son, Edward, in his ambition to follow in his father's footsteps on to the stage. Although unrecorded, help was doubtless given also to the other three girls. On 6 April 1859, all seven Elton children, wrote a joint letter to Dickens and the other Trustees, thanking them for their unwearied kindness in setting up and administering the *Elton Fund*.

> When, by the calamitous death of our Father we were left without parental care, you at once came forward, & took upon yourselves the duties & anxieties which he would have borne had his life been spared, & notwithstanding the engrossing nature of your pursuits, & the important calls you have upon your attention & time, you have continued to evince the most watchful anxiety for our welfare.
>
> Extract in Sotheby's catalogue, 6 June 1978
> quoted in the notes to Vol. 9 of the Pilgrim
> Edition of Dickens' Letters

Dickens remained friendly with Esther for the rest of his life, continuing to correspond with her even after her marriage and resettlement in Nice. He was much impressed by how she had dealt with the tragedy which had befallen her family, writing to Angela Burdett-Coutts on 17 September 1845 – 'I regard it, really as an instance of patient womanly devotion; a little piece of quiet, unpretending, domestic heroism; of a most affecting and interesting kind'. A number of accounts suggest that Esther provided the model for the character of Esther Summerson in *Bleak House*.

The case of Charles Bailey differed from that of the other victims considered here. While they had been deprived of aid and support through the death of a relative or friend in the sinking of the *Pegasus*, he had survived the wreck, but lost both his possessions and, with the death of Robinson Torry, his employment. He had, however, a story to tell, and, as his early newspaper interviews showed, a good gift of the gab. Although there is no record of his receiving further external support after the initial contributions from the people at the *Granton Hotel*, he was well positioned to apply self-help to the situation. Returning to Hull, he began to write an account of his life so far, and of how he survived this, and an earlier wreck. He concluded it with what seems a particularly modern endorsement for Carte's life belt:

> Mr. Carte's Life Belt, is a valuable article, and ought to be on board of every vessel. I have tried it in the water at Hull, and do not scruple to say, that if I could have found one on board the Pegasus, I could have swam to the shore.

The pamphlet's publication was announced in his local paper, *The Hull Packet,* on 13 October.

> A MEMOIR OF THE PEGASUS, – We are informed that a small tract has recently been published by Charles Bailey, well known as one of the survivors of the ill-fated Pegasus, containing a narrative of his life, and particularly of the events connected with the melancholy loss of that vessel. A friend, who has read the little work, commends it highly as a graphic account of a deeply interesting subject ably and artlessly related,

and eloquently appeals to the sympathies of the public on behalf of 'a man who by repeated perils and calamities of the ocean has become reduced to a state of physical infirmity, and great impoverishment.'

One thousand copies of the sixty-page pamphlet were printed. At a cost of sixpence, they sold out in Hull within a few days.

The following year, Bailey made use of his increasing fame to offer swimming lessons in the Humber. Certainly, by his endeavours Bailey was able to turn the tragedy to his own benefit, deriving an income from his experiences. When he died in the 1860s, he had provided his wife with an annuity to see her through her widowhood.

CHAPTER 18

EPILOGUE

Despite the ineffectiveness of the recommendations of both the inquest and the select committee, the *Pegasus* disaster did raise an awareness of the need for improved passenger safety, and in the months after the ship sank, a number of measures were brought to public attention, both by practical demonstration and coverage in the press.

The first invention to be publicised as a result of the disaster was the Portable Lighthouse, invented by John Robinson, a London chemist. With the co-operation of those at Bamburgh Castle, arrangements were made to carry out a trial of the apparatus at the Goldstone Rock, where the *Pegasus* went down. On Saturday, 16 September 1843, a safety boat was launched from the Castle, steered by Captain Weatherstone. The boat reached the Goldstone at eight p.m. Then:

> the composition was now ignited, and the darkness which formally prevailed was succeeded by an immense light, which illuminated the surface of the water as far as the eye could reach, rendering, besides, the position of the vessel and those on board perfectly visible and apparent to those on shore.
>
> *Berwick and Kelso Warder* 23 September 1843

The experiment was declared to be a complete success, and the *Warder* reporter stated that it was one of *the most important inventions of the century, even including the Davy lamp*. Further successful demonstrations were carried out at Berwick on the following Monday, when the light was ignited a mile out to sea from the pier head, and on the Tuesday from the Guildhall Steeple. Despite the good impression created by such demonstrations, there seem to be no records of Robinson's invention being adopted.

On 30 September 1843, the *Yorkshire Gazette* reported on the work of the *Edinburgh and Leith Humane Society*. They had already recommended the use of safety capes on ships, to help keep people buoyant. These were India-rubber inflatable capes and could be purchased for less than £1. They now sent a circular to shipping companies and owners, suggesting that all ships should carry sufficient floats for all passengers. This was to be achieved by replacing the current flock pillows in the berths by Macintosh air pillows, fitted with straps or strings to pass arms through and fasten in an emergency. Otherwise, they could be covered with a pillowcase in the same way as the flock ones. Such pillows, it was claimed, would support more than one person in the water. They also suggested that lifeboats carried cords floated with cork and made visible by white rags tied to them. These could then be thrown to passengers in the water for whom there was no room in the boats. The ships' boats themselves were to be made more buoyant by fitting foot long air cushions under the seats. In time, such ideas were to influence safety practices on ships.

A patent was also taken out by a Mr Morgan for a new type of lifeboat, and publicised in *The Times* by Captain Townsend Dance R.N. of the Royal Institution. The specification was impressive:

> These boats are so constructed as to take up scarcely any room on a ship's deck, ... any two people can get them ready for use in less than three minutes ... remarkably buoyant and elastic, though of great strength, and calculated to carry passengers through any sea, and safely land them through almost any surf; ...
>
> 18 October 1843

Any records of their actual use, however, seem to have sunk without a trace.

Alexander Gordon Carte, the Hull Ordnance Storekeeper, whose invention of the life buoy, has already been noted, embarked on a tour of British seaports during the 1840s, during which he demonstrated not only his life buoys, but also life belts, sea service rockets used to carry a line from a stranded vessel to the shore or another ship, and night signals which seem to have been similar in nature but more portable than Robinson's Lighthouse. In 1851, these contributions to maritime safety won him a silver gilt medal at the Great Exhibition.

As for the Hull and Leith Steam Packet Company, it did not have a good year in 1843. Not only was the *Pegasus* lost, but three months later, their flagship, the *Martello*, was badly damaged in a storm. The two disasters resulted in the Thompson McKay members of the Board selling their shares back to Thomas Barclay. In the aftermath of the wreck, William Pringle also resigned. His experiences on Holy Island and at the inquest must have been very stressful, and in 1844 he left to set himself up as an independent commission agent and ship broker. The remaining partners, Thomas Barclay and Robert Cook, however, drove the company forward. In 1847 it merged with the Edinburgh and Dundee Steam Packet Company, becoming the Forth & Clyde Shipping Company, and in 1852, when the company began regular sailings to Hamburg, the name was again changed to the Leith, Hull & Hamburg Steam Packet Company. Thomas Barclay, its Managing Director, died in 1853, and his place on the Board was taken by his brother Robert, whose own shipbuilding business had also expanded to become Barclay & Curle, one of the great Clyde shipbuilding companies. Tragically, Robert Cook, who had been the third founding partner in the business, was drowned in 1856, on the maiden voyage of one of the Company's new ships, the *Roslin*, returning from Stettin to Leith. His place on the Board was taken by Alexander Blackwood, who became a partner, and gave up the sea for an office role as Marine Superintendent. In 1862, James Currie joined the Company and was responsible for opening up new routes. The following year both Robert

Barclay and John Inkster, the long serving Company secretary, died, and Currie and Blackwood became the senior partners. Blackwood died at the age of eighty in 1884. The Company name was changed at the outbreak of the Second World War, becoming the Currie Line, and as such, it continued to operate into the twenty-first century.

APPENDIX

Details of the Crew and Passengers on the Final Voyage of the *Pegasus*

There follows, as far as can be ascertained, details of the men and women known to have lost their lives in the wreck of the *Pegasus*, and, for the sake of completeness, also of the six survivors. They are arranged alphabetically in three groups: the crew; the civilian passengers; and the soldiers, with their families where relevant.

Information on the people concerned has been gathered from visits to known burial places; newspaper accounts; genealogical, naval, and military websites; and family descendants.

THE CREW

AGNEW, Alexander: Second Engineer

Alexander Agnew originated from Glasgow. According to the British Merchant Seamen Register, he was born in 1811. His wife was Margaret Stewart. They are probably the Alexander Agnew and Margaret Stewart, both from the Calton area of Glasgow, recorded as being married by William Rutledge of the Glasgow Episcopal Chapel on 1 November 1830. At this time, Alexander was described as a weaver. By the time of the birth of their first daughter, Jessie Rowan, on 9 February 1833, Alexander's occupation was recorded as engineer, and the family was living in Anderston. It is possible that Alexander initially trained as an engineer to work on the new power looms which were replacing hand loom weaving in the city, but the move of the family to Anderston, a dockland area of the city, suggests that by this time he was working on ships. Certainly, he registered as a merchant seaman in Glasgow. He is recorded as serving on the *Pegasus* in December 1842. At the time of his death, accounts described him as 'very stout'. His body was never recovered.

In all, he and Margaret had six children: Janet, d.o.b. unclear; Jessie, b. 1833; Isabella b. 13.4.1835; George b. 25.5.1837, d. 3.12.1839; Margaret Alloway b. 15.11.1839; and Alexander, b. 1843 in Leith. By the 1841 Census, the family were living in Catherine Street, still in the Anderston area. When the *Pegasus* went down, only four children were said to be alive. By this time the family had moved to Leith and were still there in 1846 when Jessie married. By 1851, however, widow Margaret returned to the Calton area, and became a power loom weaver, as did daughter Isabella. Son,

Alexander, became a fabric designer. On 18 May 1851, Margaret married again – to John Dempster, a cloth dyer. In 1876, she died from liver disease.

BROWN, George: Seaman

According to newspaper reports, George Brown was married, and came from Leith, but with such a common name, it has proved impossible to identify any further definite information. Three seamen with that name, and from Leith, appear on the Seamen's Register. His body was never recovered.

BROWN, William: First Mate SURVIVOR

William Brown was said to came from Leith and was unmarried. According to the evidence he gave to the Parliamentary Commission, he had joined the crew of the *Pegasus* eighteen months previously, so presumably at the very end of 1841 or the beginning of 1842. Between the 1841 census and the Seamen's Register, there are at least three possible candidates, but no way of identifying which is correct.

When William was found by the *Martello*, he was in a boat nearly insensible from cold and exhaustion. His account, pieced together from various newspapers, was as follows:

> His watch should have commenced at midnight, but the steersman, Johnston was late in calling him, and when the ship struck, he was still getting dressed in his quarters. He went straight to the Captain on the bridge. He saw the ship was on the Goldstone Rock. The weather was calm, and he estimated the ship's speed to have been seven to eight miles. He heard the Captain order the paddles to be backed. When the vessel sank, he and the Captain were standing nearly together on the paddle-box. She went down head foremost, till about half of her hull was under water. She then violently righted herself, the stern going down also, and in this manner settled at the bottom. He was drawn under water with the suction of the ship. When he rose again to

the surface, he saw the master swimming. The sea was covered with other people from the ship; there were shrieks and prayers on every side, and every so often someone sank below the surface – a most fearful scene. He took hold of a piece of floating wood, too small to take his weight, but it helped him rest and swim. Then he saw one of the boats full of water and succeeded in getting into it. He laid his piece of wood across the boat, to steady her and so he drifted till about five in the morning, when he saw the *Martello*. Though much exhausted, he managed to make himself heard, and was immediately taken on board, where every attention was paid to him.

Following the wreck, William was transferred to serve on the Hull and Leith Steam Packet Company's *Glenalbyn*, but there is no record of how long he remained with that ship. His life thereafter is obscure. It is possible that in 1881, he was the pensioner in the Royal Alfred Aged Merchant Seaman Institution at Dartford, described as a Mercantile Mariner Mate, aged 71, born in Glasgow.

CAMPBELL, Daniel: Fireman/Coal Trimmer SURVIVOR

Daniel Campbell was said to have belonged to Leith, but according to the Seamen's Register was born in Sutherland in 1803. He first registered as a seaman at Glasgow. No further personal information has been identified. Following the sinking, he was found standing upright in the swamped ship's boat, and described as being 'in a state of frigid insensibility, with the film of death overspreading his eyes'. He was rescued by the Holy Island pilot, George Markwell. He was said to have been revived by being given 'some spirits'. As he came to, his first response was to ask about the state of the engine fires. His only account of events was given to the Inquest at Berwick, and recorded in the *Berwick Advertiser* 26 August 1843:

Left Leith at half-past five o'clock on the evening of the wreck. Was on duty till 8. Called out again at 12. At half-past twelve the vessel struck her general speed was at the rate of 7 or 8 knots, an hour. She would go faster with wind, and tide in her favour, but not beyond 10 miles an hour. Got to the Bass about 8 o'clock. In such weather as there was on the night of the wreck, the vessel might make 8 or 9, but witness does not think she could make 10 knots an hour. Saw a blue light fired before he got into the small boat. The boats were lowered before he saw them. Got into one of them by slipping down the tackle. She was full of people. Saw she was likely to be swamped, and got aboard again. Jumped overboard and swam about for ten minutes or so. Got into the boat again after she had been swamped. Saw no rockets fired. Not sure who was on the bridge at the time the vessel struck. Saw one person and afterwards the Captain on it. Witness, while in the boat, did not hear him give any orders. Did not see him when he (witness) came on deck. Saw second mate.

No records have been found of his life, after surviving the sinking.

DOWELY (DOWIE), Andrew: Ship's apprentice

Andrew Dowely came from Kinross. He is probably the Andrew Dowie born there on 19 August 1827 to James Dowie, a weaver, and his wife Margaret Sinclair. William Hood, the ship's chief engineer recorded that after the sinking, when he was supporting himself on the gangplank, Andrew joined him there, and clung on till about three a.m., when he lost his grip and drowned. His body was never recovered.

HOOD, William: Chief Engineer SURVIVOR

William Hood's origins are not clear, but he seems to have been born in about 1800. He was living in Anderston Glasgow, in November 1829, when he married Mary McCall, who came from Strathaven in Lanarkshire. Together they had five surviving children – Agnes, b. 24.7.1830; Mary, bap. 27.4.1832; Charles, bap. 3.7.1836; Euphemia, b. 23.6.1839; Jean (Jane), b. 7.2.1841.

William was entered on the Seamen's Register at Glasgow in 1835 and is recorded as second engineer of the *Pegasus* in December

1842. After the loss of the *Pegasus*, he transferred to the *Martello*, where he served as second engineer. Thereafter details are very limited. His wife, Mary died in the 1850s, prior to the marriage of their son Charles in 1858. William was still alive and described as an Engineer in 1861 when daughter Euphemia married. There is no certain record of his death.

HOWARD, Louisa: Ship's Stewardess

Louisa Howard appears to have been the third child of Robert Howard, a Ships' Chandler of Black Friar Gate, Hull. She was born on 18 February 1823. In 1841, aged fifteen, she was recorded as a servant in Christopher Avery's Inn in Fish Street, Mytongate, Hull. Her uncle, Joseph Samuel Howard, was a noted doctor in Mytongate, so he may have helped her secure this job. The range of tasks expected of a pub servant would certainly have been a good preparation for a stewardess's work on a coastal steamer, and she would be familiar with the shipping trade from growing up in the Chandler's house and shop. There is no record of when Louisa joined the crew of the *Pegasus*, or of any activity on the ship, until the report of the wreck. At that time, she was described as being about five feet four inches high, and broad across the shoulders. Charles Bailey's own account described how he pushed Louisa off, when in the water she tried to grab his hand, and a place on the plank he was holding. Her body was recovered by North Sunderland fishermen on 5 August 1843 and taken to Bamburgh Castle. She was identified from the laundry marks on her clothing, and the Bamburgh Castle Land Agent, Robert Smeddle, arranged for her burial in Bamburgh Churchyard on 12 August 1843. This was recorded in the church register – 'Body of a female found drowned, supposed to be Louisa Howard. Supposed to belong to the ship *Pegasus*'.

JOHNSTONE (JOHNSON), John: Seaman

John Johnstone was said to have come from the Orkneys, and to have been married, but there were no children. Johnstone is a very common Orkney name, and it has not proved possible to identify John any more precisely. Up until the change of watch on the *Pegasus* on the night of the wreck, he had been at the helm of the ship, and so probably bears part of the responsibility for the ship being off course. On his way to his cabin when the watch changed, he woke the mate, William Brown. John's body was never recovered.

KNARESBOROUGH, William: Fireman

At the time of the accident, William was described as the brother of a Hull Coal Merchant. This seems to have been Michael Knaresborough. In the 1841 Census, Michael gave his birthplace as Ireland, so presumably William was also Irish. It was probably William's body which the divers recovered from the forehold on 14 August 1843. If so, he was buried in the graveyard at Holy Island. (See also William McCoombs below).

MARSHALL, Robert: Ship's Cook

The newspapers reported that Robert Marshall came from Leith. Nothing further has been found about him. Robert's body was never recovered.

McCOOMBS, William: Ship's Fireman

According to the Seamen's Register, William McCoombs was born in Hull in 1814, and was recorded as a coal man on the *Pegasus* in December 1842. It is possible that it was his, and not William Knaresborough's body (see above), which the divers recovered. If so, he was buried in the Holy Island graveyard.

MELVILLE, Robert: Seaman

According to the Seamen's Register, Robert Melville was born in Leith in 1804, and was thirty-one when he was entered on the Seamen's Register at Leith in 1835. He was an experienced seaman, having served on the *General Graham of Alloa* (apparently from 1826 to 1835); the *Frankfort Packet* (December 1835); the *Duke of Buccleugh* (June 1837); the *Hawk* (August 1838); and the *Columbus* (July 1839), before joining the *Pegasus*. On 23 November

1826, he married Isabella Chalmers in Leith, and they had one son, Robert, born and baptised 25 October 1827. (Newspaper accounts of the tragedy refer to there being four children, but no record can be found of any others). On the night of the wreck, Robert had taken the helm at the midnight change of watch. At the inquest, William Hood described him as 'an experienced man; had often steered the vessel through the Fairway; and was, in the best of the witness's knowledge, perfectly sober'. Robert's body was never recovered.

MILLER Alexander: Ship's Captain

According to the Seamen's Register, Alexander Miller was born in Leith in 1809. On 3 February 1831, he was married to Margaret Loutit by the Reverend Peter Petrie, minister of South Leith Chapel. Alexander and Margaret had one son, also Alexander, born 4 May 1833. Sometime in the next eight years, Margaret must have died, for on 17 June 1841, Alexander married Margaret Edmond in the parish church of South Leith. From its inscription, his silver watch, which was recovered, seems to have been given to him as a wedding present. At this time Alexander's address was given as No. 10 Shore, Leith. He was appointed captain of the *Pegasus* in February 1841, having previously served as mate, and before that had commanded a Leith smack, *Trusty*, sailing between Leith and London from 1835 onwards.

Alexander was last seen standing on the larboard paddle-box, making no effort to save himself, and then swimming in the water when the ship went down. His body was recovered by the herring boat *Thomas and Anne*, of Spittal, about half a mile east of Berwick pier, on 15 August 1843. It was identified by William Pringle, the ship's agent, from the clothing and marks on the body, viz. a sailor's blue jacket, brownish grey trousers, a lavender waistcoat, a chamois leather shirt, a flannel vest, his waist belt, the name markings on his stockings, a faint tattoo of his name on his left arm, and a 'medical blister' on his left breast.

At the time of his death, Alexander's estate was valued at £300. His son went on to train as a cork cutter in Edinburgh, but by 1856 he was working, first as a letter carrier and then as a sorter for the Post Office.

MILLER, Thomas: Second Mate

Thomas Miller was the captain's brother, and unmarried. According to the Seamen's Register, he was born in Leith in 1814/15. He is recorded as serving on the *Earl of Hopetoun* in 1836, and thereafter seems to have joined his brother's crew on the *Trusty*, sailing between Edinburgh and London. There is no definite record of when he joined the *Pegasus'* crew, but most likely following the sacking of Benjamin Beaumont, after the smuggling case in 1842. It was thought that he had been on the bridge with Alexander when the *Pegasus* struck the Goldstone Rock. As the ship was sinking, Thomas and William Hood made common cause, throwing a loose spar of wood overboard and then leaping into the water to grab it. That was the last sighting of Thomas. His body was never recovered.

PARKER, George: Ship's Steward

Newspaper reports from the time of the sinking described George Parker as coming from Hull, but it has not proved possible to find any further information about him. His body was never recovered.

TAYLOR, George: Ship's Carpenter SURVIVOR.

George Taylor is a fairly common name so the identification which follows is not certain. Most likely George Taylor was born in the Orkneys, probably on Birsay, in about 1795, the son of William Taylor, a farmer and his wife, Ann, nee Johnston. On 12 June 1823, when he was described as a carpenter, he married Christian Rendall in Kirkwall. They had eight children – George bap. 1.6.1824; John bap. 9.6.1826; Mary bap. 27.2.1829; Ann bap. 2.6.1829; William bap. 2.7.1833; James bap. 2.9.1835; Peter bap. 29.7.1838; and Grizzel, born 1840. At some point between 1835 and 1838, the family moved from Orkney to Leith, and George became a ship's carpenter. There is no record of when he joined the crew of the *Pegasus*, but when the ship was going down, he lashed himself to the mast, where he was joined by Robert Hildyard (q.v.). They were rescued from there by the crew of the *Martello*. After the wreck, George appears to have continued working as a ship's carpenter. In the 1860s the family moved to North Junction Street, Leith, and it was there that George's wife, Christian died on 1 January 1872 of apoplexy. George himself died of cancer in the family house on 3 June 1873.

CIVILIAN PASSENGERS

C AFTER A NAME INDICATES A **CABIN** PASSENGER AND **S**, A **STEERAGE** PASSENGER

AIRD, George (S)

George Aird was the fifth child of George Aird and his wife Elisabeth Burt, born in 1814. His father was a very successful businessman. When he married George's mother in 1805, he was simply a labourer, but by the time of his son's birth, he had become a grocer and spirit dealer in Edinburgh's High Street. From there, he moved his business to the Grassmarket, where, between 1817 and 1821, he went to considerable pains to get permission to build a new stone shop front. In the 1830s, he moved again to the more prestigious New Town, setting up as a grocer, tea, wine and spirit merchant in Hanover Street in 1836, and acquiring a family home *Spring Valley*, in Morningside. By 1841, George junior had left home and was working as a 'shopman', in John Crawford's grocer's shop in Falkirk, presumably gaining more experience before returning to the family business. At the time of the shipwreck, it was said that he had been on his way to London to see a little of mercantile life, before setting up in business. The divers raised his body from the sunken ship on 27 July 1843. He was buried at St. Cuthbert's Church, Edinburgh, on 10 August 1843. The death register gave his age as twenty-six. He is commemorated on a family tombstone in East Preston Street Cemetery, Edinburgh:

> George AIRD merchant Edinburgh 10.7.1847 67; wife Elizabeth BURT 27.4.1847 66; ...
>
> only son George one of the sufferers on board steamship Pegasus wrecked between 19 and 20.7.1843 ...
>
> Find My Past – Scotland Monumental Inscriptions

ALEXANDER, Christiann[a] (S)

Christiann[a] Alexander (née McArthur) was aged about fifty at the time of the wreck, and was travelling on the *Pegasus* to visit her daughter, also Christiann, her son-in-law Robert McKinlay, a printer in Hull, and three-year-old grandson, also Robert. Her husband Robert Alexander, a Paisley weaver, whom she had married in Paisley in 1813, had died some time before 1838, when her daughter had married Robert McKinlay. Mrs Alexander herself had earned a living as a weaver's pirn winder, that is she wound the spools to fit into a weaver's shuttle. Her body was recovered and taken to Leith on the *Martello*, on 20 July 1843. There is no record of where she was buried.

BAILEY, (BAILLIE) Charles (C) SURVIVOR

Charles Bailey was born in Selby on 14 April 1804, the eldest surviving son of Robert Bailey, a sailor, and his wife, Elizabeth Everett. According to his own account, aged eleven, he was apprenticed as a sailor to Captain George Smales, and made his first voyage from Hull to Riga. He had an eventful career as a mer-

Sketch of Charles Bailey; from A Narrative of the Life of Charles Bailey

chant seaman, being shipwrecked twice in the West Indies, once in 1822 and again in 1826. In 1829 he was promoted to chief mate on a voyage to South America. On 20 June 1832, he married Catherine Barker in Hull. In 1833, he had a very successful voyage with a whaling ship. In 1836, however, he gave up ocean voyaging in favour of a job as a ferryman on the New Holland/Hull ferry, working for Mr Torry, the manager. In 1837, his son, Thomas, was born.

Charles was on the *Pegasus* in July 1843 as a companion to Mr Torry's brother, Robinson (q.v.), who had been prescribed travel as a cure for ill health. It is from Bailey's published account of the wreck of the *Pegasus* that most of the knowledge of events derives.

Following his rescue, Charles Bailey published a best-selling account of his experiences aboard the *Pegasus*, and thereafter involved himself in a range of projects related to lifesaving. He also returned to the Humber ferries, serving as the captain of one of the steamers between Hull and New Holland in the later 1840s. Among the passengers on this route were a group of workmen employed by a Hull builder, Mr Sissons, who crossed the river daily to work on a contract on the Lincolnshire side of the river. When Bailey prepared to move to the captaincy of a Grimsby/ Hull steamer in 1851, the builders clubbed together to buy him an inscribed silver snuff box, commemorating 'his great kindness and attention to them'. Charles Bailey died in the 1860s, a relatively wealthy man, and was able to leave his wife a good annuity.

BANCKS (BANKS), William (C)

William Bancks was the twenty-five-year-old son of William Bancks, originally a Birmingham Ironmonger, but one who had moved to Glasgow, probably during the 1830s. At the time of the accident, he had premises on the Broomielaw. According to the *Worcester Chronicle*, William junior had lived with his maternal uncle, Richard Allport at Bewdley for some fifteen years, where he was much involved with the Oddfellows' *Loyal Victory Lodge*. It appears that when he boarded the *Pegasus*, William was returning to his uncle's after a visit to his parents, and bringing back with him a writing desk, and a large trunk, described as a family heirloom. Papers recovered from his desk related to Canada, the Oddfellows and included copies of a periodical *The Church*. His body was never recovered.

BARNETSON, Mrs (S)

There is little certain information on Mrs Barnetson, who was also described as Miss Barnetson, and her address given both as Edinburgh and as Thurston Lodge in Suffolk, on the outskirts of Bury St. Edmunds. The Suffolk address was only published after the divers recovered her luggage, suggesting that this was her destination, but not necessarily her home. It is recorded that the divers recovered some very valuable luggage belonging to her, but no list of its contents survives. The valuable luggage appears slightly at odds with her status as a steerage passenger. Her body was never recovered.

BARTON, Maria (C)

Maria, age twenty-six, was the third daughter of the surgeon, Dr. Zephaniah Barton of Market Rasen, Lincolnshire. She was returning home following a visit to Edinburgh, on which she

The Barton Family Gravestone, Market Rasen

had been accompanied by Field Flowers (q.v.), the son of the Rector of Tealby, Lincolnshire. There they had collected Field's sister Fanny (q.v.) from Miss Eliza Banks' Boarding School in Edinburgh, together with a friend, Miss Hopton (q.v.), and were now, as a party, returning to Lincolnshire. Miss Banks appears to have been the link to the members of this party. She herself was a Lincolnshire woman, the daughter of John Banks, Rector of Bratoft, and former Master of Boston Grammar School. It seems likely that it was these Lincolnshire links which prompted the Rector of Tealby to send his daughter to school in Edinburgh. Isabella Hopton also was said to have been a pupil there, and to have been travelling to Market Rasen, presumably to stay with Maria. Possibly, in the past, Maria too had attended the School. Some accounts state that Maria had been staying with Miss Banks before returning home. When Maria's body was found, she was clutching the body of the boy, William Elliott (q.v.). She is buried in the family vault at Market Rasen. The family gravestone includes:

MARIA, WHO PERISHED FROM THE
WRECK OF THE 'PEGASUS' OFF HOLY
ISLAND, THE 19TH OF JULY, 1843,
AGED 27 YEARS.

BLACK, Alexander (S)

Alexander Black of Dunbar (age c.59) had been a soldier in the 94th Regiment of Foot, enlisting in Edinburgh in 1811, and seeing service in the Peninsular Wars. He left the army when the regiment was disbanded in 1818. At the time of the wreck, Alexander was, according to the newspapers, a *lawyer*. Checking the 1841 Census, however, he is shown as a *sawyer*, a more likely trade. At that time, he was living with three sons, William (23), George (17) and John (13) in Dunbar. He travelled on the *Pegasus* in July 1843 to take a petition to the Commissioners of Chelsea Hospital, presumably hoping to become a Chelsea Pensioner. His body was recovered by a foreign fishing boat and landed at Holy Island on 24 August 1843. The body was described as being well dressed in black, with three £1 notes in the watch pocket. He was buried in the graveyard on Holy Island.

BRIGGS, Sarah (C)

Aged forty-two, Sarah Briggs was the daughter of Christopher Briggs, a Merchant in Hull. By the time of the accident, he was described as of 'independent means'. Sarah earned her living as a governess and in 1841 is recorded as being with the Walker

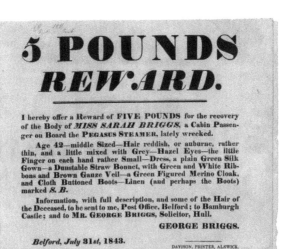

Reward Poster for Sarah Briggs
Northumberland Archives NRO ZMD-167-22-118

family in Royal Circus, Edinburgh. At the time of the wreck, however, *The Hull Packet* suggested that she had been employed by the Elphinstone Family, which would accord with the initial Es described as decorating her workbox, which may have been a leaving gift from them. A *Reward for Information* notice issued by her lawyer brother George, and now in the Northumberland Archives, provides a detailed description of her. The work box, which also had her name on the lid, was washed ashore, and the divers recovered her trunk from the ship. Despite her brother's endeavours, her body was never recovered.

BROWN, John (S)

John Brown was a painter from Elgin, where his father still lived. He also had a brother in Edinburgh. He was married. No indication has been found as to why he was travelling on the *Pegasus*. His body was recovered on 9 August 1843. When found he was carrying 28s.10½d, a silver watch, a penknife, a tobacco box, and two letters from which the addresses of his father and brother were gleaned. He was buried on Holy Island.

COLQUHOUN, James (John) (S)

James Colquhoun (age c.22) came from Paisley, where he was involved in the cloth industry. His father, also James, was a bleacher, and in 1841, the family – James senior, Margaret his wife, James junior, his wife Agnes and their four-month-old son, another James – were living at 17 Bridge Street, Paisley. In 1843, James was sailing on the *Pegasus*, en route to Norwich to deliver some textile machinery. On 9 August 1843, his body was recovered by the Revenue Cutter and brought to Mr Smeddle at Bamburgh Castle. Several letters found on his body identified him as a bleacher in Bridge Street, Paisley. Later accounts described him as the 'Manager of the Shawl Washing and Calendaring[22] Establishment' there. He was buried in Bamburgh churchyard. The textile machinery he was delivering, though badly damaged by its immersion in salt water, was recovered by the divers and sent back to Paisley. James had a posthumous son, born on 3 February 1844, yet another James, as the first son died of scarlet fever in 1844. James' widow, Agnes, and the new baby moved back to live with her parents, Robert and Agnes Spier, at Saucel, Renfrewshire.

CONNELL, Wetherspoon (S)

The only definite record of this passenger is the entry for 27 September 1843 in Bamburgh Parish Church Burial Register – *The body of a male aged 25 supposed to be Wetherspoon Connell, supposed to be wrecked in the Pegasus.*

It seems likely that he was the Wetherspoon Connell, born on 18 September 1819, to Robert Connell, a hand loom weaver, and his wife Mary Graham in Glasgow. Wetherspoon, the eldest child, grew up to be a handloom weaver like his father. There is no information as to why he was on the *Pegasus*. The body was recovered off Seahouses on 26 September 1843.

---

22 Calendaring – a way of finishing material.

EASSON, Mungo (S)

Mungo Easson was the fifth child of a Perthshire farmer, William Easson, and his wife, Isabel Aitken. William died in 1840. His brother, Robert Easson was a grocer in Dundee, and three of Mungo's brothers joined their uncle as grocers and spirit dealers there, and accounts of the sinking link Mungo to them. Mungo's oldest brother, David, however, became a gardener on the Camperdown estate, on the outskirts of Dundee. In later years, David became first the Land Steward, and then the Factor for the whole estate. Mungo, who was described as a gardener at the time of the wreck, almost certainly began his training with David at Camperdown. Newspaper accounts say that he was travelling on the *Pegasus* in furtherance of his career. Possibly a position had been found for him on an estate with Camperdown connections, such as the Philips of Warwickshire.

Mungo's body was recovered near the wreck by a French fishing boat on 15 August 1843. His clothing was described as a check shooting coat, green tartan trousers, Wellington boots, two waistcoats – the under one yellow cassimere, the upper black, a satin stock, and unbleached cotton drawers. In his pockets were – 17s. 4d. in coins, a £1 Bank of Aberdeen note, and a silver watch. After nearly a month in the water, his features were much defaced. Remarkably, he was able to be identified by the watch paper in the back of his watch. The watchmaker who had carried out the work

Mungo Easson's Gravestone, Holy Island

was contacted, and from his records he was able to identify the watch as belonging to Mungo. He was buried on Holy Island, where his tombstone, near the entrance to the Priory, is still visible, although part of the inscription is eroded.

The full inscription was recorded in 1854, when the Berwickshire Naturalists visited Holy Island:

> Erected in memory of Mungo Easson, from Dundee, aged 23 years. He perished on board the steamer Pegasus when wrecked off Holy Island on her passage from Leith to Hull, on the morning of the 21st July, 1843. His body, which is here interred, was found near the scene of the wreck, and brought on shore by a French fishing boat, after having been three weeks in the water.
>
> History of the Berwickshire Naturalists' Club Vol VII
>
> published January 1876.

EDINGTON, Mrs Caroline (C)

Caroline Edington was the daughter of Alexander Findlater, Collector of Excise for Glasgow, noted among other things for his friendship with the poet Robert Burns. She was born in the Gorbals area of Glasgow at the beginning of 1811, to Alexander's wife, Catharine Anderson. On 20 August 1841, she married James Edington of 9, Bath Street, Glasgow, an Iron Merchant and Commission Agent, twenty-three years her elder. Her husband, and her half-brother, Alexander Nisbet, a naval surgeon, were in London at the time of the wreck, and presumably Caroline was travelling to meet them. Both men came to Bamburgh in an attempt to find out what had happened. James did not remain long there but returned to Glasgow. Alexander, however, remained in Northumberland throughout August in the hope that Caroline's body would be recovered. From his reward notice, a picture of Caroline emerges. Her trunk and a satin and fur cloak were recovered from the wreck, but her body never was. Nevertheless, her death was recorded on a Findlater tombstone in Glasgow's North Street Burial Ground (now built over). It detailed the death of Alexander Findlater's sisters, before continuing:

FIVE POUNDS
REWARD.

A REWARD OF FIVE POUNDS will be paid for the recovery of the Body of the late *MRS. EDINGTON*, lost in the PEGASUS STEAMER; Age 28 years—Height about Five Feet—Figure Small—Hair auburne, long, and thick— Linen marked either *C. O. Edington* or *C. O. Findlater*, or perhaps with initials only, *C. O. E.* or *C. O. F.* Communications to be addressed to me, Post Office, Belford.

ALEXANDER NISBET.

Belford, July 29th, 1843.   DAVISON, PRINTER, ALNWICK.

Reward Poster for Mrs Edington
Northumberland Archives NRO ZMD-167-22-119
(her printed age differs from her birth date)

Also in Memory of
Alexander Findlater
Died 3 Decr. 1839 aged 85 years, and of
Mrs Caroline Oliphant Edington
his daughter
Lost at Sea 19th July 1843

Information from Alexander Findlater

ELLIOTT, James Richard, and William Bowen (C)

James Elliott (38) was a lawyer practising with his father John, in Rochdale, Lancashire. He was returning home from visiting his brother, Captain William Elliott, in Dundee, and with him he brought his young nephew, William, aged six. Presumably the boy was making a family visit to meet his Aunt Hannah, his young cousins, John (4) and Jane (3), and see his grandfather John. James and William had left Dundee by the steamer *Modern Athens* on the Wednesday morning, before joining the

Pegasus in the afternoon. From Hull, they would have planned to use the onward canal and rail links to Rochdale – a great adventure for the little boy.

The Reward for Information notice (see page 135) provides a good picture of James. His body was picked up by a fishing boat from Holy Island near the sand ridge at Goswick, on 15 August 1843. Since the body lacked both shoes and a neckerchief, the newspapers of the day concluded that he had been in bed when the ship struck. His coat, hat and portmanteau were all recovered from the sea, and the divers brought up his carpet bag from the wreck. He was buried at Holy Island, where his badly eroded headstone can still be seen. The inscription on it was recorded when the Berwickshire Naturalists visited Holy Island in 1854.

James Richard ELLIOTT Gravestone, Holy Island

Sacred to the memory of James Richard Elliott, of Rochdale, Lancashire, Attorney-at-law, who was lost in the wreck of the Pegasus steamer, on the 20th July, 1843, and interred here on the 19th of the following month, in the 36th year of his age.

History of the Berwickshire Naturalists' Club Vol VII

published January 1876

SACRED
TO THE MEMORY OF
JAMES RICHARD ELLIOTT,
OF THIS TOWN ATTORNEY AT LAW,
WHO WAS WRECKED IN THE PEGASUS,
OFF THE FERNE ISLANDS, JULY 20ᵀᴴ1843,
AND INTERRED AT HOLY ISLAND,
AUGUST 19ᵀᴴAGED 36 YEARS.
ALSO OF
HIS NEPHEW, WILLIAM BOWEN,
SON OF CAPᵀ ELLIOTT, 37ᵀᴴ REGᵀ
WHO WAS LOST AT THE SAME TIME
AGED 6 YEARS.
FIAT DEI VOLUNTAS.

Elliott memorial plaque
Photograph courtesy of Graham Knox and Norman Frisby

William Bowen Elliott's parents were Captain William Elliott of the 37th Foot, now retired on half pay, but previously a special Justice of the Peace in Jamaica, and Mary Grizzel Bowen, the daughter of a Jamaican plantation owner, Joseph Bowen. William junior was born in Jamaica, but the family were living at *Grayfield*, Dundee, in 1843. When his body was recovered, it was in Miss Barton's (q.v.) arms. William was buried at St. Chad's Church, Rochdale, where his and his uncle's death is recorded on a marble plaque.

ELTON, Edward William (C)

Mr Elton, a cabin passenger, was the most famous victim of the *Pegasus* wreck. A noted Shakespearian actor and player manager, he and his company were returning to London from a month's engagement at the *Adelphi Theatre*, Edinburgh, before touring in Yorkshire. Born Edward William Elt in 1794, he had been articled to be a solicitor. Having acquired a taste for acting at school, however, he joined a company of strolling players in the early 1820s and adopted the name Elton. He rapidly received considerable acclaim in the provinces, though rather less so in London. He also worked on behalf of less fortunate actors, becoming one of the founder members, Chairman and Treasurer of the General Theatrical Fund Association, which offered sup-

Edward William Elton
Illustrated London News 5 August 1843

port to those experiencing hardship. The news of his drowning caused a sensation, not least because he left behind seven orphan children. Elton had separated from his first wife, Elizabeth, in the early 1820s, shortly after the birth in hospital, of his second surviving daughter, Rosa. Accounts are confused, but it appears that Elizabeth suffered mental problems, and contemporaries emphasised that Elton should not be blamed. Subsequently he formed a union with Mary-Ann Sprattswill, an actress who seems to have used the stage name Pratt. The other five children were the result of this union. Mary-Ann died of jaundice in February 1840 – according to some accounts she was pregnant at the time. Elizabeth died of apoplexy in February 1843. Although Mr Elton's stage costumes etc., and his personal belonging were recovered, his body was never found.

FETTIS, Mrs (S)

All that is known of Mrs Fettis, is that her address was given as Palmer's Buildings, West Nicholson Street, Edinburgh.

FLOWERS, Field and Fanny (C)

Field (13) and Fanny Maria (11) were the children of the Rector of Tealby in Lincolnshire, the Reverend Field Flowers. Fanny had been a pupil at Miss Banks' Boarding School at 45 Moray Place in Edinburgh, and was returning home to Tealby, having had to spend the first part of the summer holiday at the school, recovering from measles. Maria Barton (q.v.), a family friend, had

Reward Poster for Field & Fanny Flowers
Northumberland Archives NRO ZMD-167-22-138

travelled up to collect her, bringing with her Fanny's brother, Field. It was said that when Fanny was much younger, her mother had rescued her from a pool in the Rectory garden, and from then on, her brother Field was particularly protective of her. The lives of the children were known to a wider audience, as her father had included stories about them in *The Children's Friend*, a monthly religious magazine for young people, to which he contributed.

After the wreck, Field's body was recovered by French fishermen on 12 August 1843, and then buried on Holy Island. Although some clothes, and carpet bags belonging to the children were found, as was Field's silver watch, Fanny's body was never recovered. She must have been an engaging child, however, as her teacher of French from the school, Monsieur A. F. Guillerez wrote a 90-line poem, in French, commemorating her death[23]. Both children were described on a Reward notice and are recorded on an eroded gravestone in Holy Island Churchyard.

IN MEMORY

OF

FIELD FLOWERS

SON OF THE REVEREND FIELD FLOWERS

AND FRANCES HIS WIFE

OF TEALBY VICARAGE LINCOLNSHIRE

AGED 13 YEARS

WHO WAS DROWNED ON THE 19TH OF JULY

1843 WHEN THE STEAMER PEGASUS

WAS WRECKED OFF HOLY ISLAND

ALSO FANNY MARIA HIS SISTER

WHOSE BODY WAS NOT FOUND

---

23 Originally published in France, it appeared in the *Caledonian Mercury* 4 September 1843 and the *Berwick and Kelso Warder* 9 September 1843.

The Flowers' Gravestone from an early
Lindisfarne Priory postcard

HILDYARD, (HILLIARD) Robert (S) SURVIVOR

Robert Augustus Hildyard, born 20 October 1819, was the second son of a Beverley clergyman, William Hildyard, and his wife, May Hett. Both Robert and his elder brother, William John, became merchant seamen. In April 1843, Robert is recorded in the Seamen's Register as being second mate on the ship *Candidate* and in his evidence to the parliamentary committee, he said that he had sailed to New South Wales and the East and West Indies.

Why Robert was travelling from Scotland is unknown – possibly a ship he was serving on had docked on Clydeside – but presumably he was returning to Beverley at the time of the wreck. His first account of events after his rescue, given to the *Edinburgh Evening Courant*, and published 22 July 1843, was as follows:

> I was lying down below at the time the vessel struck. I sprang upon deck, ran forward, and looking down the forecastle, saw that the vessel was fast filling with water. The Captain and mate

were then standing on the cross bridge; and the order was given, I believe, by the Captain, to reverse the engine, which was done. I then went aft, and saw the passengers, men and women, rushing into the boats. I dropt down into the boat on the starboard side (the same as that Baillie was in), but seeing that the boat was overcrowded, and that no one appeared to know how to manage her, I thought it would be better to remain in the ship, and I clambered up the vessel's side again. This was before the boat swamped. I went forward again and saw that the vessel was fast sinking. Several passengers were then round the Captain asking him what was to be done, but I am not certain of the answer he made. The Captain appeared to be very cool and collected. I then took off my hat, boots, and stocking, and cut off some two or three fathoms of rope, intending to lash myself with it to any floating thing I might fall in with. I went forward again. The Captain was still on the bridge talking to the mate. The last words I heard him utter were, as the vessel went down, 'Great God, look at this.' Before this, two rockets and a blue-light had been burnt by order of the mate as signals of distress. When the vessel went down I was standing on the after part of the paddle-box. I went down with her, and was about half a minute under water. While down, I was clutched by the legs by one or two drowning people; but I managed to extricate myself from them. When I rose to the surface the top part of the funnel was disappearing; the stern of the ship was still above water, and I observed some women upon it, shrieking and praying. The first thing I laid hold of was the accommodation ladder; I got astride of it, and pushed it as well as I could to the foretopmast, which was then about eight feet above the water. The mainmast had no top: before the ship sunk I saw a woman climb up the mainmast; she would, of course, be drowned, as the mast was under the water. When I came to the topmast, I found the carpenter clinging to it. I asked him if there was room for two? he said yes. We then managed to lash the ladder across the mast with the rope I had secured, and thus both of us obtained standing-room. We were picked up about half-past six o'clock by the Martello steamer. By this time the tide had flowed so fast that only two feet of the mast was above the water; and I had stripped off the rest of my clothes, thinking that I should be driven from the mast by the advancing tide, and have to swim to the shore – a task which, as the nearest land was about three miles off, in my exhausted state I should have had little chance of accomplishing.

Perhaps his near drowning experience was enough to make Robert change his career. In the 1851 census, he was a railway clerk at Spofforth station near Wetherby. He was still working as a railway clerk, now at Carlton Miniott, near Thirsk in 1861 and 1871. He died at Carlton Minniott on 19 September 1871, aged fifty-three.

HODGSON, Thomas W. (C)

Thomas Wilton Hodgson, aged twenty-six, was the son of an Edinburgh printer, William Hodgson and his wife, Elizabeth Wilton. In 1841, Thomas was awarded the Chemistry Medal of the recently founded Queen's College in Edinburgh. His older brother William (much later to become Professor of Political Economy at Edinburgh University) was Secretary of the Mechanics Institution of Liverpool in 1841, and Thomas, described as an Engineer, was staying with him there. It may have been William's influence which led Thomas to apply for the assistant secretary-ship of *Leeds Mechanics' Institution and Literary Society* in the early summer of 1843. He was successful, and after visiting his father in Edinburgh, Thomas boarded the *Pegasus* on 19 July, en route to his new post in Leeds. It was reported that he was due to deliver his first lecture there the following Tuesday, 25 July. Thomas's body was found floating off Bamburgh rocks on 18 August 1843, and he was buried in the graveyard there that evening.

HOPTON, (HOPETOUN) Isabella (C)

The information recorded on Isabella is contradictory and confusing. Some accounts describe her as a school friend of Fanny Flowers (q.v.) but others state that she was thirty and travelling to Market Rasen. She seems to have had some connection with Miss Banks' Boarding School, and as Maria Barton lived at Market Rasen, it is possible that she was in fact Maria Barton's friend. Had both women been Miss Banks' pupils in earlier years?

Only two Isabella Hoptons feature in the Edinburgh 1841 census – the first was 25 and a servant in the house of the noted Scottish Architect, William Burn; the second, the five-year-old daughter of William Hopton, one of a number of Hopton Clockmakers in Edinburgh at that time. Perhaps the lady who died in the wreck was sister to the clockmakers?

Her body was recovered and buried in Bamburgh Parish Church graveyard on 13 August 1843.

HUNTER, James (S)

James Hunter was the second surviving son of David Hunter, a tinsmith and ironmonger, of 17 Howe Street, Edinburgh, and his wife Catharine Miller. James was also a tinsmith and was said to be going to London to learn more about the business. His body was found floating near the scene of the wreck on 25 August 1843, with £4 or £5 on his body. He was buried two days later on Holy Island.

INNES, Mr (S)

Nothing is known of Mr Innes, save that the divers recovered the body of a man of that name from the wreck on 8 August 1843.

JOHNSTON, Ralph (S)

Ralph Johnston (26) was the youngest son of William Johnston, who had farmed Renton Barns near Grantshouse, Berwickshire. Ralph qualified as a surgeon, having been apprenticed in Berwick and/or Edinburgh. He went out to New Zealand for some time. He is probably the Ralph Johnston recorded as Surgeon Superintendent on the emigration ship *London*, which sailed for New Zealand on 13 August 1840, arriving at Port Nicholson on 12 December that year. It is not clear whether he returned to Britain on the *London,* in the company of a party of Maori dancers, or came back on a later ship. At the time of the wreck, it was said that he had 'returned some time ago'. He was on the *Pegasus* travelling to join friends in Yorkshire when the wreck occurred. His body was never recovered.

LAIDLAW, George (S)
Nothing is known of George, save that James Miller of Fisherrow recovered a clothes box belonging to him on 27 July 1843. It was claimed by his father whose address was given as Minnyhive, (Moniaive) Glencairn, Dumfriesshire. No body was found.

MACKENZIE, The Reverend John Morell (C)
John Morell Mackenzie (37) originated from St. Neots, Huntingdonshire. He had been a good academic student, and after boarding school, trained for the ministry at the dissenting seminary at Wymondham and then at Glasgow University. His first charge was at Poole, but in 1837 was called to be a Pastor to the Independent Chapel in Nile Street, Glasgow. While there, he married Joanna Trotter, the daughter of the late Lieutenant General Alexander Trotter of Fairmilehead, Edinburgh. Then, in 1839, he was offered a post as Lecturer in Biblical Criticism and Church History at the Congregational Theological Academy in Glasgow, where he seems to have been very successful. In the following years, as well as his work at the Academy, he visited the Isle of Bute to provide support for a growing Congregational church there.

In the summer of 1843, John and Joanna had taken a holiday at Portobello on the Lothian coast. When the holiday was over, it had been arranged that he would travel south to visit his sister and parents, and to give a sermon in Bedford. He chose to sail on the *Pegasus*, rather than the more modern *Martello*, to avoid travelling on the sabbath. As the *Pegasus* was sinking, he gained distinction by refusing to try and save himself, despite being a strong swimmer, and instead gathered other passengers to him and prayed with them until the ship went down.

The *Memoir* of him published in 1845/6 described him as below middle height, with a tendency to corpulence, but with very attractive features 'which easily won the favourable opinion of the most casual acquaintance'. Another account in the *Congregational Magazine*, talks of his musical skills, generous nature and kindly sense of humour.

After the wreck, his body was recovered on 7 August 1843 by the Bamburgh Castle boat. It had been intended that his body should be buried in his wife's family vault at Greyfriars Churchyard in Edinburgh, but it was too badly decomposed to be moved. Instead, he was buried at Bamburgh Parish Church on 11 August 1843. The grave is marked by a broken pillar monument with the following inscription:

TO THE MEMORY OF
THE REV. JOHN MORELL MACKENZIE, M.A.,
LATE PROFESSOR OF BIBLICAL CRITICISM
AND CHURCH HISTORY
IN THE GLASGOW THEOLOGICAL ACADEMY,
WHO LOST HIS LIFE BY THE WRECK OF
THE STEAM-SHIP PEGASUS,
OFF THE GOLDSTONE ROCK,
ON THE MORNING OF THE 20TH JULY, 1843.
THIS STONE, THE FRAIL MEMORIAL OF WORTH,
WHICH IS IMPERISHABLE, HAS BEEN ERECTED BY
HIS WIDOW.
ENDOWED WITH TALENTS OF THE HIGHEST
ORDER, WHICH HE ASSIDUOUSLY CULTIVATED;
POSSESSING STORES OF VARIED AND VALUABLE
LEARNING, TO WHICH HE WAS CONSTANTLY
ADDING;

AND ADORNED WITH THE GRACES OF A
NATURALLY AMIABLE DISPOSITION AND THE
VIRTUES OF A SINCERE AND DEEP-TONED PIETY,
HE WAS HAPPY, HONOURED, AND USEFUL IN LIFE;
AND IN DEATH,
AMID CIRCUMSTANCES OF A PECULIARLY
APPALLING CHARACTER, HE AFFORDED A
STRIKING EXAMPLE OF THE POWER OF THAT
RELIGION WHICH HE PROFESSED,
TO COMPOSE AND ELEVATE THE MIND IN THE
PROSPECT OF AN IMMEDIATE ENTRANCE INTO
THE WORLD OF SPIRITS.

McLEOD, Murdoch and Ann (C)

Records for the McLeods are limited. Murdoch McLeod was probably born in the parish of Fodderty, Ross and Cromarty, in 1813, to a father of the same name. By 1840, he was working in Aberdeen as a Clerk at the Royal Mail Coach Office, in the *Royal Hotel*, Union Street, where he also lived. The hotel owner, Isaac Machrae, was also the mail contractor. On 23 March 1843, Murdoch married Ann Barnett, the daughter of John Barnett, a stonemason, in Aberdeen. Murdoch was approximately twenty-nine years old and described as short (five feet three inches) and stout, while Ann was about five feet six inches high, also stout, with dark hair and a short nose, 'rather turned up at the point'. The married couple moved into an Aberdeen house belonging to Hugh Mackay. It seems possible that the visit south, which brought them aboard the *Pegasus*, was in fact a delayed honeymoon.

Ann's body was the first of the two to be recovered, on 22 July 1843, and was buried in St. Aidan's Churchyard, Bamburgh on Wednesday 26 July 1843. Murdoch's body was recovered on 12 August 1843 and was buried that day in the same churchyard.

MARTIN, James – father and son (S)

James Martin senior was a native of Edinburgh, born about 1810. He had moved to London to work as a carpenter and upholsterer in Tavistock street by 1832, when he married Mary Wilson, a milliner, there. Mary, too was a Scot, and had grown up in Newhaven, a fishing village on the outskirts of Edinburgh, where her father was a wine and spirit merchant. It is not clear why the young people decided to move to London. Once there, however, James became one of the founding members of the *London Working Men's Association,* a group of skilled artisans, who met in James' house and campaigned for equal political and social rights. This group was the forerunner of the more widely known Chartist movement.

In 1833, James and Mary had a son, also James. A daughter, Lavinia, was born two years later, but died in 1837. By 1843, the family had moved to Great Russell Street, and James's business was in financial difficulties, probably as a result of the move from Tavistock Street. He travelled north, to try to raise funds from his friends and family in Edinburgh, taking with him his ten-year-old son, probably the first chance there had been to introduce him to his Scottish relatives. A petition, on behalf of his widow, records that he had successfully raised the necessary finance – when his body was recovered some £50 were found in his pockets – and was returning on the *Pegasus* 'in the highest spirits'. His body was picked up by Holy Island fishermen on 5 September 1843 and interred at Holy Island on the following day. The situation regarding his son was confused – one of the bodies taken to Leith on the *Martello* on 20 July 1843 was immediately claimed as being that of James junior, and sent down to London, only to be returned to Leith as 'the wrong child'. His body was never found, or if found, never identified.

The widow, Mary Martin, continued to live in Great Russell Street for the next two to three years, but in 1846, she moved to Stanhope St., when on 3 August 1846, she remarried, this time to a London Wine Merchant, George Newton, with whom she had three further children.

MILNE, William (C)

William was the 'Son' of *Wm Milne and Son, Boot and Shoe Makers to Her Majesty and the Queen Dowager, 100 George Street, Edinburgh*, although by this time his father had died. At the time of the wreck, he was approximately twenty-seven years old, and described as five feet seven inches, with black hair and a sallow complexion. His body was found floating a mile north of Emmanuel Head and was picked up by the Coldingham herring boat *Alert*, John Cormack master. He was said to be wearing a spotted black vest, brown olive coat, black and white checked trousers, a Codrington over-all, Shetland grey socks and new boots with red morocco lining. He was carrying a red pocketbook with fifteen sovereigns in one of the pockets, and loose money in his vest pocket. It was the recovery of this body which finally enabled an inquest to be held and the circumstances of the sinking of the *Pegasus* to be formally explored. Following the inquest, William's body was returned to Leith, where he was buried at Leith South Parish Church, alongside other family members.

MOXHAM, Arthur (C)

There was some confusion over which Moxham died in the wreck of the *Pegasus*. Most contemporary listings name the victim as Egbert. Egbert, however, was still alive in 1851. Presumably, Egbert had booked the cabin ticket, but the actual passenger was his older brother, Arthur. The Moxham boys were the sons of James Moxham, a Quaker schoolmaster, and his wife, Elisabeth, also a schoolteacher. They were born in Thornbury, Gloucestershire, Arthur in 1821, and Egbert in 1824. The 1841 Census shows them living with their parents in Neath, Monmouthshire. By now Arthur was a draughtsman, and Egbert an apprentice builder. By 1843, Egbert had moved to Edinburgh, possibly now training in architecture[24]. In June that year, Arthur travelled up from Wales to join his brother for a two to three week tour of the highlands and to spend some time in Edinburgh. Arthur was returning from that trip, when he boarded the *Pegasus* on 19 July 1843 and was seen off by Egbert. Arthur's body was never found, although the divers recovered a carpet bag belonging to him from the wreck.

POLIS, Mrs (S)

Almost nothing is known of Mrs Polis, a steerage passenger. Her address was listed as Stamford Street, London, and she was described as an elderly woman. A letter addressed to her was found on the body left unclaimed in the mortuary at Leith – possibly this was Mrs Polis.

PRIMROSE, William (S)

William Primrose, born in 1820, was the only son of William Primrose, an Ayrshire carpet weaver. According to a letter sent to Thomas Barclay, owner of the *Pegasus*, William junior showed a particular interest in drawing which his parents had encouraged with money they could ill afford. The problem was made worse when the father lost his sight and was unable to work. The 1841 Census shows William junior as a stonemason, now living with his parents in the Gorbals area of Glasgow. On 14 July 1843, William married an already heavily pregnant Elizabeth Laughland in the Gorbals. He must have left her almost immediately after the wedding, to catch the *Pegasus* on 19 July 1843. A letter found on his body suggests he was travelling to Stoke Rochford in Lincolnshire. During 1843, major building works were going on at Stoke Rochford Hall and village, under the direction of the Scottish architect William Burn, and it seems likely that William had been employed, or was about to be employed by him there.

---

24 The 1851 Census shows Egbert as a qualified Architect.

William's body was recovered off Holy Island by the Dundee ship, *Twin Brothers*, master, Robert Rollo, during the week beginning 20 August 1843, but was so badly decomposed that it was weighted and sunk immediately where it was found. From the body, Rollo recovered a silver watch, ten shillings and two letters which enabled the identification to be made. Following William's death, the baby was born, and William's widow and now almost destitute parents sought support from the committee formed to assist the relatives of those lost. They also received a small amount of direct financial support from Thomas Barclay – the only family for which there is a record of this happening.[25]

SCOTT, David (S)

David Scott was the eleven-year-old only son of a Paisley Shawl Manufacturer, Matthew Scott, and his wife, Elizabeth. The family business was in Causeyside, but the family had a separate house in Hamilton Street. After David's birth, his mother Elizabeth disappears from the records, and Mrs Stewart (q.v.) was employed as his nurse. In 1843, when Mrs Stewart decided to visit her son in London, she invited David to come with her to see the capital. They left Leith on 19 July 1843 on the first stage of that journey. When the wreck occurred, David made strenuous attempts to save himself, and clung to what is described as part of a skylight for several hours. Although he was dead when his body was retrieved by the *Martello*, it was still warm. The obituary for his father in 1876 (*Paisley Herald and Renfrewshire Gazette*) records that David's death 'cast a cloud over not a few of the best years of his life'.

STEWART, Mrs Catherine (S)

Mrs Stewart was the wife of Matthew Stewart of 56 Love Street, Paisley, described in the papers as an Elder in Mr Nisbet's church.

---

25 University of Glasgow Library, Archives & Special Collections UGD 255/4/17/5/5 and UGD 255/4/17/1/2

This appears to have been the Abbey Close Church, Paisley. The *Paisley Advertiser* carried a description of the lady – *Mrs Stewart was above fifty years of age, below the middle size of females, and slender. She was dressed in a kind of chocolate coloured figured gown, of cotton and woollen fabric; a white straw bonnet, with striped ribbons and black veil; black silk figured shawl; black cloth boots; and grey worsted stockings. She had three rings on her fingers; and on her person a red leather pocket-book containing a one-pound note of the Paisley Commercial Bank, with some silver.* She was visiting London to see her son, Alexander (age c.24), who was a surgeon there, living at 43 Aldersgate, and took with her David Scott (q.v.), whom she had nursed as a baby. Her reticule was recovered as well as a package addressed to her husband in Paisley, and one to herself at her son's address. Her body was never identified, and possibly never found.

TORRY, Robinson (C)

Robinson Torry was born on 26 August 1815, the eighth child of William Torry, a builder of Market Rasen, and his wife Mary Robinson. He is recorded in the 1841 census as an apprentice, in the Market Place shop and house of Richard Howe, a draper in the same town. As well as Richard Howe, his wife and child, the building housed in addition to Robinson, another draper, three further draper's apprentices, a milliner and three female servants – twelve occupants in all. Sometime in the next two years, Robinson became unwell and was recommended to travel for the good of his health. Although some newspaper accounts implied a form of breakdown, his 4x great niece has suggested that he may have suffered from tuberculosis. Given what must have been the cramped conditions he was living in, this seems very possible, and would accord with the recommendation for sea air. Robinson's older brother, James, the manager of the New Holland Ferry, arranged for one of his employees, Charles Bailey (q.v.) to accompany him on a sea voyage. At the time of the shipwreck, the two men seem to have been returning from that voyage. Robinson, however, was clearly still not in the best of health – Bailey saw that he ate just after the ship left Leith, and then put him to bed.

Later, when the ship struck the Goldstone, Bailey helped him from the cabin and got him into one of the ship's boats. When that boat capsized, Robinson seems to have been unable to help himself. His body was never recovered.

WHIMSTER, David (S)

In 1818, David Whimster was born in Kinghorn, Fife, to James Whimster, a farmer, and his wife Ann Williamson. James had served in the 79th Regiment of Foot throughout the Napoleonic wars, but became a reserve at the end of the war, classified as a half-pay Lieutenant. David was the first of his children to be born in Britain. In 1841, David and his brother Thomas were boarders with Mrs Bell in Edinburgh, and David was working as a draper with Messrs Ireland & Son on South Bridge. At the time of his death, he was recorded as very religious and amiable. He was sailing on the *Pegasus* en route to Sheffield, to be licensed as a Methodist preacher at the Methodist Conference taking place there. His death was formally recorded at the Sheffield Conference, but, sadly, his body was never recovered.

Military Passengers

On 17 August 1843, the *London Evening Standard* published a notice issued by the Adjutant General's Office, giving an account of the total loss of the **Recruiting Party** of the 96th Regiment in the wreck of the *Pegasus*. The members of the Party were named as: Lance-Sergeant Scotter, Corporal B. Dunn, Private J. Harford, and Private R. Liddell, with the Lance-Sergeant's wife and boy, seven years old, and a recruit for the 78th Regiment, named J. McDougall; also, a little girl, daughter of a soldier belonging to the 25th Regiment, now in India, who was coming with the party to Chatham, before travelling on to India, and her father, with troops being sent out there.

DUNN, Corporal B.

Bartholomew Dunn was in charge of the recruiting party for the 96th Regiment, at that time based at Chatham. The regiment was in the process of sending reinforcements to New Zealand, where fighting had broken out between the Maoris and some settlers on North Island. Dunn's recruiting party was probably intended to make up numbers, after a contingent had been sent out to New Zealand. His body was recovered in the waters off Seahouses on 26 September 1843, and buried the following day in St. Aidan's Churchyard, Bamburgh.

HARFORD, Private J.

He is recorded as one of the recruiting party of the 96th Regiment but no other certain records can be found for him. If his body was recovered, it was not identified.

LIDDELL, Private R.

He is recorded as one of the recruiting party of the 96th Regiment, but there are no other certain records for him. If his body was recovered, it was not identified.

SCOTTER, Lance Sergeant William, and family

Lance Sergeant Scotter was on the *Pegasus* as part of the 96th Regiment recruiting party, along with his wife Martha, and his son John. William was born in Ireland about 1812, and enlisted in the army in October 1831. He married Martha Harvey, in Meath in 1837, and John seems to have been born that year. In 1839, William was promoted to Corporal. In 1841, the family were based at Sheerness Barracks. No bodies which could be definitely identified as the Scotters' were ever recovered.

McDOUGALL, Neil (J)

McDougall was a new army recruit, travelling on the *Pegasus* with the recruiting party to join the 78th Regiment. There is some confusion over McDougall's name – newspaper reports and the items found on his body would identify the man as Neil, but the army records list him as J. McDougall. His body was recovered by the Bamburgh Castle boat on 9 August 1843, and he was buried two days later in St. Aidan's churchyard, Bamburgh. He was said to be carrying a Bible or Testament with his name and an inscription from Donald McInes, Sandyford Toll, Glasgow, a letter addressed to Sergeant Ross, 78th Regiment, a razor and a small two-bladed pocketknife. Before being recruited, Neil was probably the journeyman blacksmith, aged c.25 in 1841 and living in Hill Street, Glasgow.

ALLAN, Susan

Susan Allan was the daughter of a soldier in the 25th Regiment, serving in India. She had remained at home in Aberdeen with her mother. As her mother had recently died, Susan was travelling with the Recruiting Party, before accompanying the 56th Brigade out to India to join her father. Her body was never recovered.

Other soldiers: according to Mr Pringle's testimony at the Inquest, a second group of soldiers, not in uniform, some of whom had drink taken, boarded the *Pegasus* on the afternoon of 19 July 1843. There is no record of how many were in the party, but it did include a sergeant, named either Mackay or Munro; a sergeant with a heavily pregnant wife; and possibly a Captain O'Neil. There is no traceable army record for the deaths of any of this party. Possibly the two further named soldiers whose bodies were recovered were part of this group.

PEGOT, Private Graham Vernon
No military records can be found for Pegot. On 24 July 1843, a trunk belonging to Pegot was recovered off Holy Island. From the papers found in it, his address was Staines, Richmond, Surrey and he had been carrying discharge papers made out to Private 731 in the 6th Regiment of Dragoon Guards.

STEWART, W.S. Soldier 86th Regiment of Foot
No certain military records can be found for Stewart. His body was recovered with Dunn's, off Seahouses on 26 September 1843, and he was buried in St. Aidan's churchyard, Bamburgh on 27 September 1843. His identification is dependent on the entry in the Bamburgh Church register.

Unknown:
The bodies of three unidentified soldiers were recovered.

» On 4 August 1843, the body of a soldier in the uniform of the 96th Regiment, was picked up by the steamer *Vesta*. He was too disfigured for identification, but in his pockets were £3.3s.9d, a tobacco box, knife and keys. He was buried at Holy Island on Monday 7 August 1843.
» On 11 August 1843, the body of a soldier was recovered off Craster.
» On 13 August 1843, the steamer *Rapid* saw a soldier's body floating in the water, but did not attempt to recover it.

The fate of the heavily pregnant sergeant's wife is not record-ed. Some accounts say that when the wreck was first found, the body of a pregnant woman was among those taken to Leith by the *Martello*. With the exception of one elderly woman, however, all these bodies were claimed. It must be assumed, therefore, that her body too, was never recovered. Possibly the box of baby clothes which was recovered from the wreck had belonged to her.

In all, at least twenty-seven bodies were never accounted for; twenty of these bodies were never found, and a further seven, when found, were too badly damaged to be identifiable.

BIBLIOGRAPHY

Primary:

Burial Register for Holy Island, Northumberland Archives, NRO EP 136/8

Burial Register for St. Aidans Church, Bamburgh, Northumberland Archives, NRO MF 1053

Davison, William, 'Printers Proofs' Northumberland Archives ZMD 167-22-

The Leith, Hull and Hamburg Steam Packet Company, University of Glasgow Library, Archives & Special Collections MS UGD 255/4/

James Hopkirk, 'A Statistical Account of the Barony Parish of Glasgow with the principal transactions of the Heritors for the last forty years', 1827, University of Glasgow Library, Archives & Special Collections, MS Murray 636

Second Report from the Select Committee on Shipwrecks together with the Minutes of Evidence taken before them, House of Commons Parliamentary Papers online, 1843 (581), parlipapers.proquest.com

Lloyd's Register of Ships online, 1805-1868, Lloyd's Register Foundation Heritage & Education Centre, hec.lrfoundation.org.uk, archive.org

United Kingdom Merchant Navy Seamen Records, 1835-1857, National Archives, Series BT112

Papers of Herbert Hayes 1916-1945, National Library of Australia MS 738 Series 7, Elton Letters

Petition of David Smith, County Fire Officer London, National Records of Scotland, GD112/11/10/8a/26

Jottings by Sir William Fraser of his first visit to London,
September 1840, National Records of Scotland,
GS237/21/58
Ordnance Survey, 'Name Books, Midlothian', Vol. 85, 1852-
53 OS1/11/85/7

Newspapers:

Contemporary newspapers are one of the key original sources.
Over the years, original papers have been consulted in libraries
and archives across the country, now largely replaced by the online *The British Newspaper Archive* (https://www.britishnewspa-
perarchive.co.uk), although not all relevant newspapers are dig-
itised – in particular, relevant issues of the *Berwick Advertiser* and
the *Berwick and Kelso Warder* are not yet available online. A feature of nineteenth century newspapers, rather as in tweets today, good stories were copied and republished in other papers
across the country – literally from Bristol to John o'Groats, and
in Australasia, only sometimes with the original source acknowledged. The key sources for the accounts are:

Berwick Advertiser
Berwick and Kelso Warder
Caledonian Mercury
Edinburgh Evening Courant
Edinburgh Observer
Hull Advertiser and Exchange Gazette
Hull Packet
Morning Chronicle
Newcastle Courant
Newcastle Journal
Other papers with coverage of relevant local stories are:
The Era
Fife Herald
Leeds Mercury
Lincoln Rutland and Stamford Mercury
Lincolnshire Chronicle

Paisley Advertiser
Sheffield Independent
Yorkshire Gazette

Secondary:

Anon. *The Remains of the Late Rev. John Morell Mackenzie, with a selection of his Correspondence, and a Memoir of his Life,* (Edinburgh, 1845, printed for private circulation)

Anon. 'Death of Mr John Morell Mackenzie, M.A.', *The Scottish Congregational Magazine* 3/8, (1843) 408

Anon. 'Sketch of the Life and Character of the late J. Morell Mackenzie, M.A.', *The Scottish Congregational Magazine* 3/9, (1843) 409–428

Anon. *Handbook of Communication by Telegraph,* (London, 1842)

Anon. The Prayer of the Pegasus *Religious Tract Society* 133, (London 1850)

Bain, Joseph Colin, 'The Employment of the Steamship in the East Coast Trades to 1850', PhD thesis, University of St. Andrews, 1996

Backhouse, Sarah, Tuke, Samuel, eds, *The Annual Monitor for 1844, or Obituary of the members of the Society of Friends in Great Britain and Ireland for the year 1843,* (London 1844)

Bevan, John, *Another Whitstable Trade,* (Gosport, 2009)

Caledonian Maritime Research Trust, Scottish Shipbuilding Database, http://clydeships.co.uk

Campbell, Gordon A., 'Congregationalism on the Island of Bute', *Congregational History Magazine,* 8/4, (2017), 25-38

Daiches, David, *Glasgow,* (London, 1982)

Donaldson, Gordon, *Sir William Fraser,* (Edinburgh, 1985)

Gifford, Paterson, *Men of the Clyde, a Compilation* (n.p. 1995)

Greenwood, John, *Picture of Hull,* (Hull, 1835)

Greenwood, R.H., Hawks, F.W., *The Saint George Steam Packet Company 1821-1843,* (Kendal, 1995)

House, Madeline, Storey, Graham, Fielding, Kenneth J., Turner, Mary Tillotson, eds, *The Letters of Charles Dickens* ii–ix (Oxford 1969-1997)

Horne, Richard, *The Life of Van Amburgh, the Brute Tamer: with Anecdotes of his Extraordinary Pupils*, (London, 1838)

Johnson, Edgar, *Letters from Charles Dickens to Angela Burdett-Coutts 1841-1865*, (London, 1955)

Johnston, George, 'Our Visit to Holy Island in May 1854', *History of the Berwickshire Naturalists Club* 7, (1873-5), 27-52

Kotar, S.L., Gessler, J.E. *The Rise of the American Circus*, (Jefferson, North Carolina, 2011)

Maw, P., Wyke, T., Kidd, A., 'Water Transport in the Industrial Age, Commodities and Carriers on the Rochdale Canal 1804-1855', *Journal of Transport History*, 3/2 (2009), 200-228

Mendonça, Sandro, 'The evolution of new combinations: drivers of British maritime engineering competitiveness during the nineteenth century', DPhil thesis, University of Sussex 2012

Moore, John, 'Glasgow Made the Clyde', *Scotland's History* 19/2 (2019), 20-22

Murray, J., 'The Wreck of the Steamship *Pegasus* 1843', *Open History* 51, (June 1994)

Pearson, F.H., *The Early History of Hull Steam Shipping*, (Hull, 1896; facs. edn Goole: Mr Pye Books, 1984)

Post Office *Annual Glasgow Directories* (Glasgow, 1800-1870s)

Reid, Robert, *Old Glasgow and its Environs*, (Glasgow, 1864)

Russell, W. Clark, *The Ship: Her Story*, (London 1899)

Scott, Andrew, 'Reminiscences of the Glasgow Custom-House, Trade of Clyde, Steamers, &c.', *Transactions of the Glasgow Archaeological Society* 1/1 (1859)

Walton, Geri, 'Andrew Ducrow: The Colossus of Equestrians', Unique histories from the 18th and 19th centuries blog (21 Feb. 2020), geriwalton.com

BBC 'Who do you think you are?' programme with Sarah Millican broadcast 4 September 2013, YouTube uploaded 4 October 2014

Genealogical Research Websites:

Ancestry, www.ancestry.co.uk
Family Search, www.familysearch.org
Find My Past, www.findmypast.co.uk
Forces War Records, www.forces-war-records.co.uk
Scotland's People, www.scotlandspeople.gov.uk

INDEX

OF PEOPLE, PLACES, SHIPS AND KEY EVENTS

*Numbers in **bold** indicate an illustration*

225

HERZ FÜR AUTOREN A HEART FOR AUTHORS À L'ÉCOUTE DES AUTEURS MIA KAPΔIA ΓIA ΣYΓΓPA
ARTA FÖR FÖRFATTARE UN CORAZÓN POR LOS AUTORES YAZARLARIMIZA GÖNÜL VERELIM SZÍV
PER AUTORI ET HJERTE FOR FORFATTERE EEN HART VOOR SCHRIJVERS TEMOS OS AUTOR
ZÖINKÉRT SERCE DLA AUTORÓW EIN HERZ FÜR AUTOREN A HEART FOR AUTHORS À L'ÉCOUTE
AÇÃO ВСЕЙ ДУШОЙ К АВТОРАМ ETT HJÄRTA FÖR FÖRFATTARE À LA ESCUCHA DE LOS AUTORE
MIA KAPΔIA ΓIA ΣYΓΓPAΦEIΣ UN CUORE PER AUTORI ET HJERTE FOR FORFATTERE EEN HA
LARIMIZA GÖ   RE   ZÖINKÉRT SERCE DLA AUTORÓW EIN HERZ FÜR A
SCHRIJ   S O   ÇÃO ВСЕЙ ДУШОЙ К АВТОРАМ ETT HJÄRTA FÖR

The author

Jane Bowen was born in Scotland after the Second World War. She attended Schools in Dumbarton, Glasgow, and Bolton, before reading History at the University of London, and training as a teacher at Cambridge. Jane taught in Bedford, Hertfordshire and Isle of Man before she became headmistress of a school in North Yorkshire. From there she returned to Scotland to join the Schools Inspectorate where she was involved in a range of initiatives among the most interesting of which was contributing to an inspection of Child Protection arrangements. On retiring, she returned to her first love of history, wrote a history of the Belford Workhouse, and contributed to publications of her local history society. She took a course in palaeography and began researching stories of interest such as that of the Pegasus. This took on another dimension when she was invited to contribute to the BBC 'Who do you think you are?' programme with Sarah Millican.

The publisher

He who stops getting better stops being good.

This is the motto of novum publishing, and our focus is on finding new manuscripts, publishing them and offering long-term support to the authors.
Our publishing house was founded in 1997, and since then it has become THE expert for new authors and has won numerous awards.

Our editorial team will peruse each manuscript within a few weeks free of charge and without obligation.

You will find more information about novum publishing and our books on the internet:

www.novum-publishing.co.uk